/RAS
2 circ 9/01
12/01

SACRAMENTO PUBLIC LIBRARY

3 3029 03737 7611

CENTRAL LIBRARY
828 "I" STREET
SACRAMENTO, CA 95814
MAY - 1997

D0819688

AN INTRODUCTION TO FOSSILS AND MINERALS

SEEKING CLUES TO THE EARTH'S PAST

The Changing Earth Series

JON ERICKSON

Facts On File®

AN INFOBASE HOLDINGS COMPANY

AN INTRODUCTION TO FOSSILS AND MINERALS:
SEEKING CLUES TO THE EARTH'S PAST

Copyright © 1992 by Jon Erickson

All rights reserved. No part of this book may be reproduced or utilized in any form or by any means, electronic or mechanical, including photocopying, recording, or by any information storage or retrieval systems, without permission in writing from the publisher. For information contact:

Facts On File, Inc.
460 Park Avenue South
New York NY 10016

Library of Congress Cataloging-in-Publication Data

Erickson, Jon, 1948—
    An introduction to fossils and minerals : seeking clues to the
earth's past / Jon Erickson.
        p. cm. — (The changing earth)
    Includes bibliographical references and index.
    ISBN 0-8160-2587-8 (acid-free paper)
    1. Fossils. 2. Minerals. 3. Geology.   I. Title. II. Series:
Erickson, Jon, 1948– Changing earth.
    QE711.2.E75   1992
    560—dc20   91-34390

Facts On File books are available at special discounts when purchased in bulk quantities for businesses, associations, institutions or sales promotions. Please call our Special Sales Department in New York at 212/683-2244 or 800/322-8755.

Text design by Ron Monteleone
Jacket design by Catherine Hyman

Printed in the United States of America

RRD FOF 10 9 8 7 6 5 4 3 2

This book is printed on acid-free paper.

CONTENTS

TABLES IN FOSSILS AND MINERALS

ACKNOWLEDGMENTS

The author wishes to thank the U.S. Geological Survey (USGS), the National Park Service, the National Oceanic and Atmospheric Administration (NOAA), the USDA-Soil Conservation Service (SCS), and the National Museums of Canada for providing photographs for this book.

INTRODUCTION

The presence of marine fossils on dry land intrigued even the ancients. Interest in fossils grew over the centuries, and the classification of fossils became more uniform. At the same time, the science of geology progressed so that layers of sedimentary rocks could be dated according to standardized criteria. Today, advanced techniques like carbon and radiometric dating enable paleontologists to piece together the evolution of marine and land animals.

Interest in minerals and gems is also evident in the ancient world. Crystals continue to fascinate us with their symmetrical beauty while we depend on the Earth's resources for much of our energy. The rock formations in which these minerals are found reveal, layer by layer, the continual formation and erosion of the Earth's surface. There are even unusual rocks that follow the sun, glow in the dark, and reverse their direction of growth.

Geological formations can be found in most parts of the country, often within a short distance from home. This book is meant to introduce the fascinating science of geology and how it reveals the history of the Earth as told by its rocks. The text describes the components of the Earth, different rock types, and how the fossil and mineral content of the rocks are found, dated, and classified. It is also designed to aid in the location, identification, and collection of a variety of rock types, many of which contain collectable fossils and minerals. Based on the information here, amateur geologists and collectors will have a better understanding of the forces of nature and the geological concepts that will enable them to locate rocks and minerals in the field.

1

THE EARTH'S HISTORY

The Earth is a dynamic planet that is constantly changing. Continents move about, mountains rise and are eroded down to plains, seas fill up and dry out, glaciers expand and retreat, and species evolve and become extinct. These episodes in the Earth's history are divided into chunks of time, known as the geologic time scale. Each period of geologic history is distinct in its geology and biology, and no two units of geologic time were exactly the same (Figure 1).

The major geologic periods were delineated during the 19th century, principally by geologists in Great Britain and western Europe (Figure 2). Because at that time there was no means of placing actual dates on rocks, the entire geologic record was compiled by using relative dating techniques based on the fossil content of the rocks. It was not until about the middle of this century that radioactive methods of dating rocks themselves were developed, which provided absolute dates for units of relative time.

The largest divisions of the geologic record are called eras. There are four of these: the Precambrian (time of early life), the Paleozoic (time of ancient life), the Mesozoic (time of middle life), and the Cenozoic (time of recent life). Except for the Precambrian, the other eras are subdivided into smaller units called periods. There are six periods in the Paleozoic (though American geologists divide the Carboniferous into

Figure 1   A geologic time spiral depicting the geologic history of the Earth.   Earthquake Information Bulletin 214, courtesy U.S. Geological Survey (USGS)

Mississippian and Pennsylvanian periods), three in the Mesozoic, and two in the Cenozoic. Each period is characterized by somewhat less profound changes in species as compared to the eras, which mark boundaries of mass extinctions, proliferations, or rapid transformations of species.

The two periods of the Cenozoic have been further subdivided into seven *epochs*, the number of which could increase as time progresses into the future. The largest era, the Precambrian, is not subdivided, owing to the poor fossil content of its rocks, providing lesser detail about the era. It was not until the beginning of the Paleozoic, about 570 million years ago, that organisms developed hard exterior body parts, probably as a defense against fierce predators. This in turn gave rise to an explosion of life, which resulted in an abundance of fossils.

TABLE 1   THE GEOLOGIC TIME SCALE

Era	Period	Epoch	Age (millions of years)	First Life Forms
Cenozoic	Quaternary (Neogene)	Holocene	0.01	
		Pleistocene	2	Man
		Pliocene	7	Mastodons
		Miocene	26	Saber-tooth tigers
	Tertiary (Paleogene)	Oligocene	37	
		Eocene	54	Whales
		Paleocene	65	Horses Alligators
Mesozoic	Cretaceous		135	
	Jurassic		190	Birds Mammals Dinosaurs
	Triassic		240	
Paleozoic	Permian		280	Reptiles
	Carboniferous	Pennsylvanian	310	
				Trees
		Mississippian	345	Amphibians Insects
	Devonian		400	Sharks
	Silurian		435	Land plants
	Ordovician		500	Fish
	Cambrian		570	Sea plants Shelled animals
Proterozoic			700	Invertebrates
			2500	Metazoans
			3500	Earliest life

Era	Period	Epoch	Age (millions of years)	First Life Forms
Archean			4000	Oldest rocks
			4600	Meterorites

Figure 2   Type locations for geologic periods: (1) Cambrian, (2) Ordovician, (3) Silurian, (4) Devonian, (5) Carboniferous, (6) Triassic, (7) Jurassic, (8) Cretaceous, (9) Tertiary, (10) Quaternary.

THE PRECAMBRIAN ERA

The first 4 billion years, or about nine-tenths of geologic time, comprises the Precambrian, the longest and least understood era of Earth history. The Precambrian is subdivided into the Archean *eon* (time of initial life), 4.6 to 2.5 billion years ago, and the Proterozoic eon (time of earliest life), 2.5 to 0.6 billion years ago. The boundary between the Archean and Proterozoic is somewhat arbitrary and reflects major differences in the characteristics between rocks older than 2.5 billion years and those younger than 2.5 billion years. The Archean was a time when the Earth's interior was hotter, the crust was thinner and therefore more unstable, and crustal plates were more mobile. The Earth was in a great upheaval and subjected to extensive volcanism and meteorite bombardment, which probably had a major effect on the development of life early in the planet's history.

When the Earth was about half a billion years old, most of the radioactive elements that heated the mantle and kept it in a fluid state decayed into stable daughter products, and the Earth's interior gradually began to cool. This created a more permanent crust composed

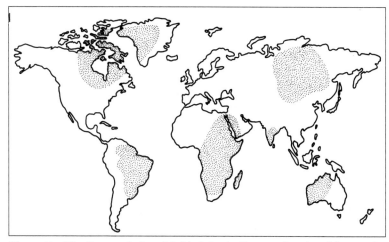

Figure 3   The Precambrian shields (shaded) comprise the oldest rocks on Earth.

of a thin layer of basalt embedded with scattered blocks of granite, or "rockbergs." These combined into stable bodies of basement rock, upon which all other rocks were deposited. The basement rocks formed the nuclei of the continents and are presently exposed in broad, low-lying, domelike structures called shields (Figure 3).

Dispersed among and around the shields are greenstone belts comprising a jumble of metamorphosed or recrystallized sediments and lava flows that were caught in the squeeze between two colliding continents. The rocks, which are tinted green due to the presence of the mineral chlorite, have been used as evidence that plate tectonics, the shifting of plates on the Earth's crust, operated as early as the Archean. Ophiolites, which are slices of ocean floor shoved up on the continents by drifting plates, as much as 3.6 billion years old, were also caught in the greenstone belts. A number of ophiolites contain ore-bearing rocks that are important mineral resources the world over. Because greenstone belts are essentially Archean in age, their disappearance around 2.5 billion years ago marks the end of the Archean eon.

The Proterozoic eon, 2.5 to 0.6 billion years ago, was a shift to calmer times as the Earth matured from adolescence to adulthood. When the eon began, as much as 75 percent of the current continental crust had formed. Continents were more stable and were welded together to form a single large supercontinent. Marine life during the Proterozoic was highly distinctive from that of the Archean and represented considerable biologic advancement.

The global climate of the Proterozoic was cooler, and the Earth experienced its first major ice age roughly 2 billion years ago. Following a second major ice age, which occurred around 700 million years ago, there was an explosion of new species, representing nearly every major group of marine

Figure 4 Glacial landscape high on the south flank of the Uinta Mountains, Duchesne County, Utah. An unnamed ice-sculptured peak at the head of Rock Creek Basin looms above a morainal ridge in the foreground. Photo 136 by W. R. Hansen, courtesy USGS

life. This set the stage for the Phanerozoic eon, or the time of later life, which comprises the Paleozoic, Mesozoic, and Cenozoic eras. Also, for the first time, fossilized remains of animals became abundant, due to the evolution of lime-secreting organisms that constructed hard shells.

By the beginning of the Proterozoic, most of the material that is now locked in sedimentary rocks was already at or near the surface. Archean rocks also were eroded and redeposited. Sediments derived directly from primary sources are called *wackes.* However, most Proterozoic wackes were composed of sandstones and siltstones derived from Archean greenstones. Another common Proterozoic rock was a fine-grained metamorphosed rock called quartzite, derived from the erosion of siliceous grainy rocks such as granite and arkose, a sandstone that contains abundant feldspar.

Conglomerates, which are consolidated equivalents of gravels, were also abundant in the Proterozoic. Nearly 20,000 feet of Proterozoic sediments were found in the Uinta Range of Utah, which is the only major east-west trending mountain range in North America (Figure 4). The Montana Proterozoic belt system contains sediments over 11 miles thick. The Proterozoic is also known for its terrestrial red beds, so named because the sediment grains were cemented with iron oxide, which colored the rocks red. Their appearance, around 1 billion years ago, indicates that the atmosphere contained substantial amounts of oxygen, which oxidized the iron similar to the way steel rusts in the open air.

The weathering of primary, or parental, rocks during the Proterozoic also produced solutions of calcium carbonate, magnesium carbonate, calcium sulfate, and sodium chloride, which in turn precipitated into limestone, dolomite, gypsum, and halite (see Glossary). These minerals are thought to be mainly chemical precipitates and not of biologic origin. The Mackenzie Mountains of northwest Canada contain dolomite deposits more than 1 mile thick. Carbonate rocks such as limestone and chalk, produced chiefly by the deterioration of shells and skeletons of simple organisms, became much more common during the latter part of the Proterozoic, between about 700 and 570 million years ago, whereas during the Archean they were relatively rare due to the scarcity of lime-secreting organisms.

During the Proterozoic, the continents were composed of odds and ends of Archean cratons, which are ancient, stable rocks in continental interiors. Several cratons were welded together to form central Canada and north-central United States (Figure 5). Continental collisions continued to add a large area of new crust to the growing proto–North American continent. A major part of the continental crust underlying the United States from Arizona to the Great Lakes to Alabama formed in one great surge of crustal generation around 1.8 billion years ago that has been unequaled on the continent. This possibly

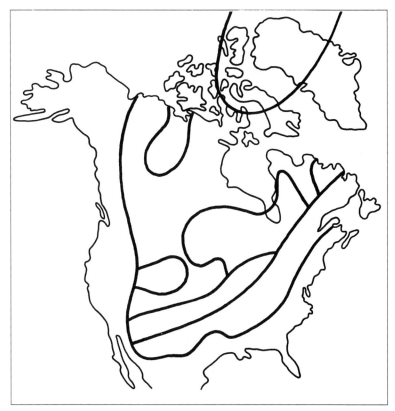

Figure 5   The cratons that constitute North America.

resulted from greater tectonic activity and crustal generation during the Proterozoic than during any subsequent time of Earth history.

Toward the end of the Proterozoic, around 570 million years ago, a super-continent located near the equator broke apart into as many as four major continents, although they were configured differently than they are today. The breakup produced some 12,000 miles of new continental margin, where vast carbonate belts formed. This extended shoreline, which provided more habitat area, might have played a major role in the explosion of new species by the time the Proterozoic came to a close.

THE PALEOZOIC ERA

The Paleozoic era, which spans from about 570 to about 240 million years ago, was a time of intense growth and competition in the ocean and, later, on the land, producing widely dispersed and diversified species. By the middle of the era, all major animal and plant phyla (groups of organisms that share the same general body plan) were already in existence. The earliest period of the Paleozoic is called the Cambrian, named for the Cambrian mountain range of central Wales, where sediments containing the earliest known fossils were found. Thus, the base of the Cambrian was once thought to be the beginning of life, and all previous time was known as Precambrian.

The Paleozoic is generally divided into two time units of nearly equal duration. The lower Paleozoic consists of the Cambrian, Ordovician, and Silurian periods, and the upper Paleozoic consists of the Devonian, Carboniferous, and Permian periods. The first half of the Paleozoic was relatively quiet in terms of geologic processes. There was little mountain building, volcanic activity, glaciation, and extremes in climate. The land was divided into two mega-continents. The northern landmass was called Laurasia and included what is now North America, Greenland, Europe, and Asia. The southern landmass was called Gond-

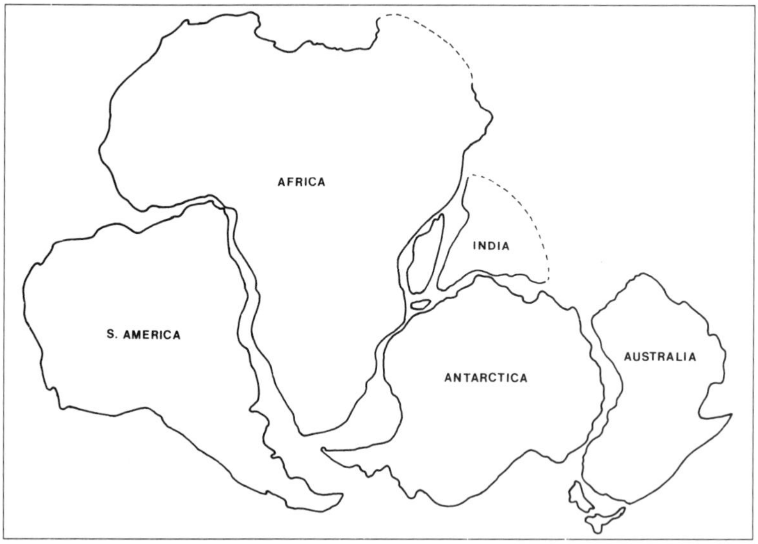

Figure 6 The configuration of the southern continents that composed Gondwana.

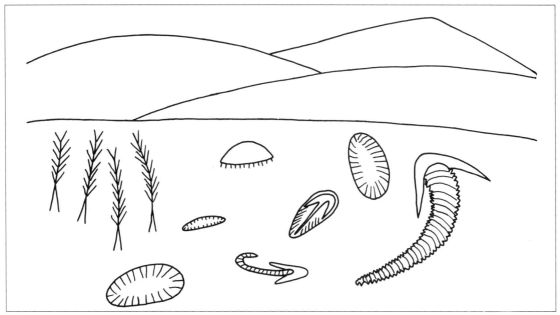

Figure 7   Late Precambrian Ediacara fauna from Australia.

wana and included what is now Africa, South America, Australia, Antarctica, and India (Figure 6).

The two megacontinents were separated by a large body of water called the Tethys Sea. Into this flowed thick deposits of sediments washed off the continents, and their accumulated weight formed a deep depression in the ocean crust, called a geosyncline. The continents were lowered by erosion, and shallow seas flowed inland, flooding more than half the landmass. The inland seas and wide continental margins along with a stable environment allowed marine life to flourish and spread throughout the world. Early geologists were often puzzled as to why the ancient rocks were devoid of fossils, and then, suddenly, abundant fossils appeared in rocks at the base of the Paleozoic the world over. There are several reasons why fossils were so abundant at the base of the Cambrian, including the development of hard body parts, which fossilize by replacement with calcium carbonate or silica; rapid burial, which prevented attack by scavengers and decay by oxidation; long periods of deposition with little erosion; and large populations of species.

Prior to the Cambrian, organisms possessed only soft body parts, which decayed rapidly when the animal died. Thus, only traces of their existence were left behind in the form of impressions inscribed on rocks. Numerous impressions of strange extinct species were found in the Ediacara formation of southern Australia that dated around 670 million years old (Figure 7). This was about the time when the great Precambrian ice age came to an end. It was the worst ice age on Earth, when nearly half the land surface was covered with ice. When the ice retreated and the seas began to warm, life took off in all directions. Unique and bizarre creatures thrived, and the Cambrian saw the highest percentage of experimental organisms, animals that evolved unusual characteristics, than any other interval of Earth history. As many as 100 phyla existed, whereas today there are only about a third as many living phyla.

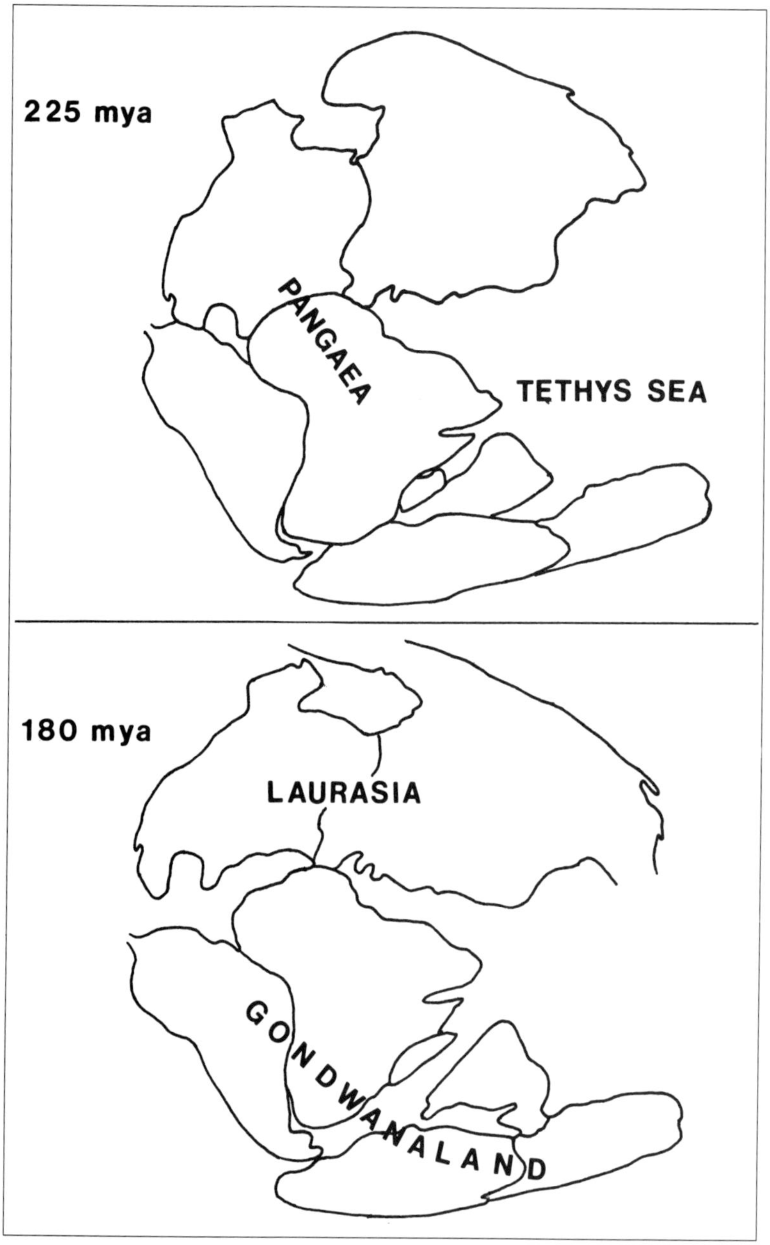

The second half of the Paleozoic followed on the heels of another ice age, which occurred during the Silurian, when Gondwana wandered into the South Polar region around 400 million years ago. As sea levels dropped lower and the continents rose higher, the inland seas departed and were replaced by great swamps. In these areas, vast coal deposits accumulated during the Carboniferous, which comprises the Mississippian and Pennsylvanian periods in North America. During the Permian, all the interior seas retreated from the land, an abundance of terrestrial red beds accumulated, and large deposits of gypsum and salt were laid down. During the latter part of the Permian, around 240 million years ago, Gondwana and Laurasia converged into a single crescent-shaped

Figure 8a   The breakup and (Figure 8b) drift of the continents.

supercontinent, called Pangaea, that extended practically from pole to pole.

The sediments that accumulated into thick deposits in the Tethys Sea were later squeezed by continental collisions and uplifted into mountain belts, including the Ouachitas and Appalachians of North America and the ancestral Hercynian Mountains of southern Europe. In addition, the collision between Siberia and Russia created the Urals. The closing of the Tethys Sea eliminated a major barrier to the migration of species from one continent to the other, and they dispersed to all parts of the world.

As the continents continued to rise and the ocean basins continued to deepen, the land became dryer and the climate grew colder. Continental margins were less extensive and narrower, placing severe restrictions on marine habitat. By the time the Paleozoic came to a close, the southern continents were in the grips of a major ice age, about 240 million years ago, and the worst extinction event the world has ever known left the planet devoid of 95 percent of all known species. In effect, the Earth was almost as devoid of life at the end of the Paleozoic

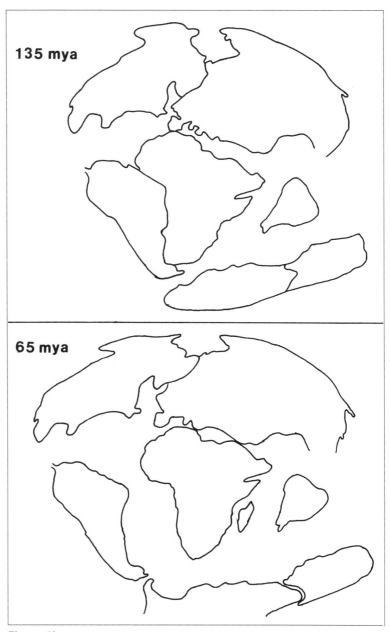

135 mya

65 mya

Figure 8b

Figure 9   A red bed formation on the east side of the Bighorn Mountains, Johnson County, Wyoming. Photo 1016 by N. H. Darton, courtesy USGS

as it was at the beginning of the era.

THE MESOZOIC ERA

The Mesozoic era consists of the Triassic, Jurassic, and Cretaceous periods and spans from about 240 to about 65 million years ago. The Earth was in the process of recovering from a major ice age and the worst extinction event in geologic history. Animals that were immobile and could not migrate to better habitat and those that developed specialized life-styles and were unable to adapt to a changing environment experienced the worst extinction. Those able to survive into the Mesozoic differed markedly from their close relatives that were left behind.

Thus, the beginning of the Mesozoic was a sort of rebirth of life, and 450 new families of organisms came into existence. However, instead of the introduction of entirely new body styles, as in the early Paleozoic, the beginning of the Mesozoic saw only new variations on already established themes. Therefore, there were much less experimental organisms, and many of the lines of today's species evolved.

At the beginning of the era, all the continents were consolidated into a supercontinent; about midway through the era, they began to break up; and at the end of the era, most were well on their way to their present locations (Figures 8a and 8b). The breakup of Pangaea created three major bodies of water: the Atlantic, Arctic, and Indian Oceans. The climate was exceptionally mild for an unusually long period of time. One group of animals that excelled during these exceptional conditions were the dinosaurs. Some reptilian species returned to the sea while others took to the air. They occupied nearly every corner of the globe, which is why the era is generally known as the "age of the reptiles." Then suddenly, for unexplained reasons, the dinosaurs disappeared along with 70 percent of all other species after having dominated the planet for some 140 million years.

When the Triassic period began about 240 million years ago, there existed a single large continent and a single large ocean. The great glaciers of the previous ice age melted, and the seas began to warm. The energetic climate eroded down the high mountain ranges of North America and Europe. Reef building was intense in the Tethys Sea, and thick deposits of limestone and dolomite laid down by lime-secreting organisms were later uplifted to form the Dolomite Alps of northeastern Italy.

In North America, terrestrial red beds covered the Colorado Plateau and a region from Nova Scotia to South Carolina (Figure 9). Red beds were also common in Europe. The wide occurrence of red sediments might have resulted from large amounts of iron supplied by intense igneous activity around the world. Air bubbles trapped in ancient tree sap indicated a greater abundance of oxygen in the atmosphere, which was responsible for oxidizing the iron to form hematite, so named because of its bloodred color.

In Siberia, there were great lava flows and granitic intrusions. Also, extensive lava flows covered South America, Africa, and Antarctica. Southern Brazil was covered by some 750,000 square miles of basalt, constituting the largest lava field in the world. These great outpourings of lava probably reflected enormous crustal movements brought on by a vigorous plate tectonics. By the close of the Triassic, North and South America separated; India, nestled between Africa and Antarctica, began to separate from

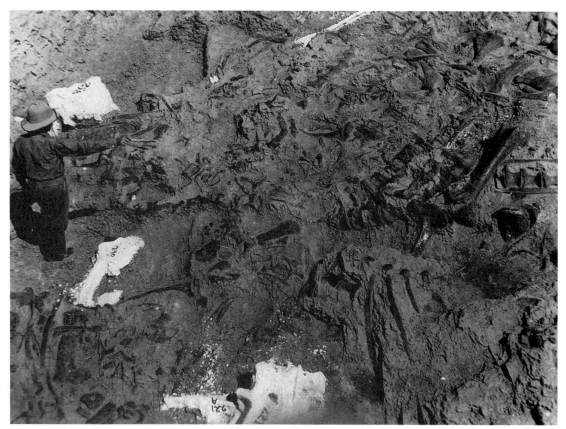

Figure 10   A dinosaur boneyard at the Howe Ranch quarry near Cloverly, Wyoming. Photo 198 by G. E. Lewis, courtesy USGS

Gondwana; and a great rift began to split apart North America and Eurasia, eventually forming the North Atlantic.

During the Jurassic period, which began about 190 million years ago, the Tethys Sea still provided a wide gulf between the northern and southern landmasses and continued to fill with thick deposits of sediment. An interior sea, called the Western Interior Cretaceous Sea, flowed into the west-central portions of North America, and accumulations of marine sediments eroded from the cordilleran highlands to the west (sometimes known as the ancestral Rockies) were deposited on the terrestrial red beds of the Colorado Plateau, forming the Morrison formation, well known for its abundant dinosaur bones (Figure 10).

In South America, great floods of basalt, 2000 feet or more thick, covered large parts of Brazil and Argentina. Vast quantities of basalt also flowed in Africa, Antarctica, and from Alaska to California, accompanied by massive granitic intrusions such as the huge Sierra Nevada batholith of California which is about 400 miles long and 50 miles wide. Because of the effects of seafloor spreading, whereby new oceanic crust was created at midocean ridges while old oceanic crust was destroyed in deep-ocean trenches, the crust of the Pacific Basin is no older than Jurassic in age (Figure 11).

During the Cretaceous period (from the Latin creta meaning "chalk"), which began about 135 million years ago, huge deposits of limestone and chalk were laid down in Europe and Asia. Seas invaded Asia, South America, Africa, Australia, and the interior of North America. Into the latter were deposited thick layers of sediment, which are presently exposed as impressive cliffs in the western United States. The Appalachians, which were an imposing mountain range at the beginning of the Triassic, were eroded down near the base by the Cretaceous. The rim of the Pacific Basin became a hot bed of geologic activity, and practically all mountain ranges facing the Pacific Ocean and island arcs along its perimeter developed during this period.

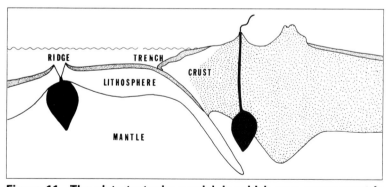

Figure 11 The plate tectonics model, in which new ocean crust is generated at spreading ridges and old ocean crust is destroyed in subduction zones, or trenches, which then moves the continents around the face of the Earth.

Toward the end of the Cretaceous, North America and Europe were no longer in contact except for a land bridge created by Greenland to the north. The Bering Strait between Alaska and Asia narrowed, creating the Arctic Ocean, which was practically landlocked. The South Atlantic continued to widen, with South America and Africa separated by more than 1500 miles. Africa moved northward and began to close the Tethys Sea, leaving Antarctica, which was still joined to Australia, far behind. Meanwhile, India began to cross over the equator and narrowed the gap between southern Asia.

As Antarctica and Australia moved eastward, a rift developed between them that would eventually separate the two continents. The Earth rifted open on the west side of India, and massive amounts of molten rock poured onto the landmass in less than half a million years. It blanketed much of west-central India, known as the Deccan Traps, in layers of basalt hundreds of feet thick. This deposit may have had a major impact on the climatic and ecologic stability of the planet, resulting in the extinction of the dinosaurs.

THE CENOZOIC ERA

The Cenozoic era began about 65 million years ago and extends to the present. It is divided into the Tertiary period, which occupies most of the era, and the Quaternary period, which covers the last 2 million years. (Both terms are carried over from the old geologic time scale in which the Primary and Secondary periods represented ancient Earth history.) The pronounced unequal lengths of the two periods is the result of the unique sequence of ice ages that began about 2.4 million years ago.

Most European and many American geologists prefer to subdivide the Cenozoic into two nearly equal time intervals. The first is the Paleogene period from 65 to 26 million years ago and includes the Paleocene, Eocene, and Oligocene epochs. The second is the Neogene period from 26 million years ago to the present and includes the Miocene, Pliocene, Pleistocene, and Holocene epochs. Regardless of the time scale one uses, the Cenozoic is generally regarded as the "age of mammals."

Early in the Cenozoic, about 60 million years ago, a great rift appeared between Greenland and Norway. About the same time, Greenland began to separate from North America. Except for a few land bridges that were exposed from time to time, animals were largely restricted from migrating from one continent to another. At times, Alaska connected with east Siberia across the Bering Strait, closing off the Arctic basin from warm-water currents, resulting in a large accumulation of pack ice. The Mid-Atlantic Ridge, of which Iceland is a surface expression, began to occupy its present position midway between North America and Eurasia during the Miocene, about 16 million years ago.

North and South America remained separated until the Panama Isthmus was uplifted during the Pliocene, about 4 million years ago. This precipitated a lively exchange of species between the two continents. Prior to the connection of North and South America, powerful currents flowed from the Atlantic into the Pacific, carrying an assortment of unusual animals from the West Indies to the Galapagos Islands, which are volcanic islands

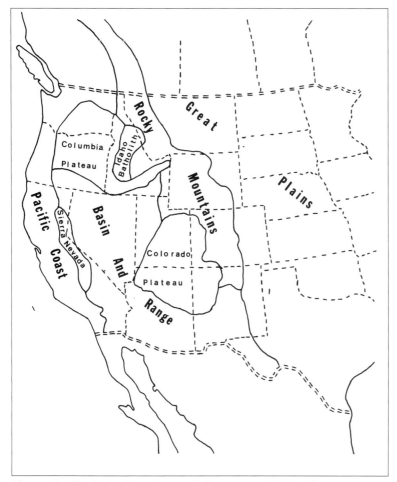

Figure12   Geological provinces of the western United States.

of the East Pacific Rise spreading ridge system, lying some 300 miles west of Ecuador. South America was temporarily connected to Antarctica by a narrow, curving land bridge, which was instrumental in the migration of marsupials across the continent to Australia. Antarctica separated from Australia in the Eocene, about 40 million years ago, drifted over the South Pole, and acquired a thick sheet of ice, obliterating practically all life.

The Cenozoic is also known for its intense mountain building, and highly active tectonic forces established the geologic provinces of the western United States (Figure 12). In the Pacific Northwest, paramount changes were felt all along the Pacific Coast of North America. Volcanic activity was extensive, and great outpourings of lava covered Washington, Oregon, and Idaho. Miocene-age basalts of the Columbia River Plateau covered 200,000 square miles and in some places were 10,000 feet thick. In the late Cenozoic, the tall volcanoes of the Cascade Range from northern California to Canada erupted in a single great profusion. There was also extensive volcanism in the Colorado Plateau and Sierra Madre regions.

The Laramide orogeny (mountain-building episode), beginning about 80 million years ago and ending some 40 million years later, pushed up the Rocky Mountains, which extend from northern Mexico into Canada. During the Miocene, the large part of western North America was uplifted, and the entire Rocky Mountain region was raised over 3000 feet in elevation. Numerous parallel faults sliced through the Basin and Range province, between the Sierra Nevada and the Wasatch Mountains, during the Oligocene, producing about 20 north-south trending mountain ranges.

Crustal movements in the Oligocene, about 25 million years ago, brought about changes in relative motions between the North American plate and the Pacific plate, which created the San Andreas Fault system that runs through southern California (Figure 13). As another result of crustal movements, Baja California split off from North America and opened up the Gulf of California. On the other side of the world, Arabia split off from Africa by a continent rift that flooded and became the Red Sea.

About 50 million years ago, the Tethys Sea narrowed as Africa approached Eurasia and began to close off entirely during the Miocene some 20 million years ago. Thick sediments that had been accumulating for tens of millions of years folded over, and the folded sediments formed great belts of mountain ranges on the northern and southern continental landmasses. The entire crusts of both continental plates, up to 10 miles thick, were buckled upward and formed the central parts of the range.

This episode of mountain building, called the Alpine orogeny, ended around 26 million years ago and marks the boundary between the Paleogene and Neogene periods. It raised the Alps of northern Italy, the Pyrenees on the border between Spain and France, the Atlas Mountains of northwest Africa, and the Carpathians in east-central Europe. The collision of India with southern Asia, around 40 million years ago, uplifted the tall Himalayan Mountains and the broad Tibetan Plateau, most of which lies 3 miles above sea level. The mountainous spine that runs along the western edge of South America forming the Andes Mountains continued to rise throughout much of the Cenozoic due

Figure 13 The San Andreas Fault in southern California. Photo 194 by R.E. Wallace, courtesy USGS

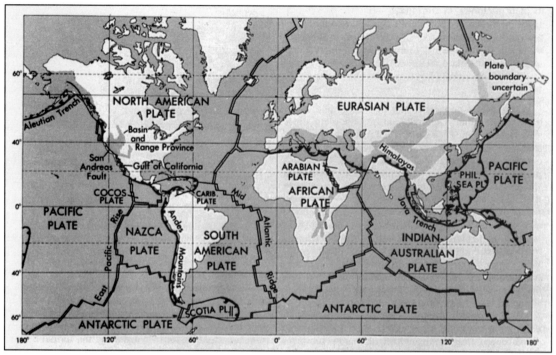

Figure 14 **The lithospheric plates that compose the Earth's crust.** Courtesy USGS #626

to the subduction, or slipping, of the Nazca plate beneath the South American plate. The melting of the subducting plate fed magma chambers (volcanic reservoirs) with molten rock and caused numerous volcanoes to erupt in one fiery outburst after another (Figure 14).

THE ICE AGE

The Pleistocene epoch, which began about 2.4 million years ago, saw a progression of ice ages, followed by short, warm interglacial periods, similar to the one we are living in. The last ice age began about 100,000 years ago, intensified about 75,000 years ago, peaked about 18,000 years ago, and retreated about 11,000 years ago (Figure 15). The ice took considerably longer to build to its fullest extent than it took to melt away to what is left at the poles today.

In North America, there were two main glacial centers. The largest ice sheet, called the Laurentide, spread out from Hudson Bay and reached northward to the shores of the Arctic Ocean and southward to bury all of eastern Canada, New England, and much of the northern half of the midwestern United States under a sheet of ice up to 2 miles thick. A smaller ice sheet, called the Cordilleran, originating in the Canadian Rockies, engulfed western Canada, parts of Alaska, and small portions of the northwestern United States. Ice sheets buried the mountains of Wyoming, Colorado, and California, and rivers of flowing ice connected them with mountains in northern Mexico.

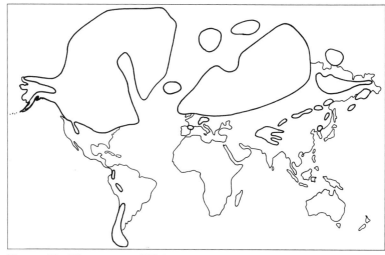

Figure 15   The extent of Pleistocene glaciation.

TABLE 2   CHRONOLOGY OF THE MAJOR ICE AGES

Time (years)	Event
2 billion	First major ice age
700 million	The great Precambrian ice age
230 million	The great Permian ice age
230–65 million	Interval of warm and relatively uniform climate
65 million	Climate deteriorates, poles become much colder
30 million	First major glacial episode in Antarctica
15 million	Second major glacial episode in Antarctica
4 million	Ice covers the Arctic Ocean
2 million	First glacial episode in Northern Hemisphere
1 million	First major interglacial
100,000	Most recent glacial episode
20,000–18,000	Last glacial maximum

Time (years)	Event
15,000–10,000	Melting of ice sheets
10,000–present	Present interglacial

There were also two major glacial centers in Europe. The largest ice sheet, called the Finnoscandian, radiated from northern Scandinavia and covered most of Great Britain and large parts of northern Germany, Poland, and European Russia. A smaller ice sheet, called the Alpine, was centered in the Swiss Alps and covered parts of Austria, Italy, France, and southern Germany. In Asia, the ice sheets occupied the Himalayas and parts of Siberia. In the Southern Hemisphere, only Antarctica had a major ice sheet. Smaller ice sheets existed in the mountains of Australia, New Zealand, and the Andes of South America. Throughout most of the world, alpine glaciers occupied mountains that are presently ice free.

The accumulation of ice lowered the sea level by as much as 350 feet, which substantially extended the shoreline of the continents seaward. It also brought several land bridges to the surface, which aided the migration of animals and humans into various parts of the world. Adaptations to the cold climate allowed certain species of mammals to thrive in the ice-free regions of the northern lands. Giant mammals, like the mammoth, saber-tooth cat, and giant sloth roamed many parts of the Northern Hemisphere that were free of glaciers.

One of the most dramatic climate changes in the history of the Earth occurred during our present interglacial, known as the Holocene epoch, which began about 11,000 years ago after the glaciers retreated. The collapse of the ice sheet and the subsequent warming of the climate left many puzzles, such as an unusual occurrence of hippopotamus bones in the deserts of Africa. During a wet period between 12,000 and 6000 years ago, some of today's African deserts were covered with large lakes. Lake Chad, which lies on the border of the Sahara desert, appears to have swelled over 10 times its present size. Swamps, long since vanished, once harbored large populations of hippopotamuses and crocodiles, whose fossil bones now bake in desert sands.

2

CLUES TO THE PAST

Fossils have been known from ancient times, and the first to speculate on the origin of fossils were the early Greeks. The Greek philosophers recognized that seashells found in the mountains were the remains of once-living creatures. Although Aristotle clearly recognized that certain fossils like fish bones were the remains of organisms, he generally believed that fossils were placed in the rocks by a celestial influence. This astrologic account for fossils maintained popularity throughout the Middle Ages. During this time, competing fossil theories included the idea that fossils actually grew in rocks, were discarded creations, or tricks of the Devil to deceive humans about the true history of the world. Fossils were also thought to be the creations of Mother Nature in a playful mood.

It was not until the Renaissance period and the rebirth of science that alternative explanations for the existence of fossils based on scientific principles were sought. By the 1700s, most scientists began to accept fossils as the remains of organisms because they closely resembled living things rather than merely inorganic substances. The early 19th-century English engineer and geologist William Smith made the most significant contribution to the understanding of fossils when he proposed the law of faunal succession, which stated that rocks could be placed in their proper time sequence after a study of their fossil content. Therefore, fossils did not occur randomly but in a determinable order from simple to complex. This law became the basis for the establishment of the geologic time scale and the beginning of modern geology.

KEYS TO THE HISTORY OF LIFE

One of the major problems encountered when exploring for fossils of early life is that the Earth's crust is constantly rearranging itself, and only a few fossil-bearing formations have survived undisturbed over time. Therefore, the history of the Earth as told by its fossil record is not completely known because of the remaking of the surface, which erases whole chapters of geologic history. Yet, the study of fossils along with the radiometric dating of the rocks that contain them has constructed a reasonably good chronology of Earth history.

Among the oldest fossils found on Earth are the remains of ancient microorganisms and stromatolites (Figure 16), which are layered structures formed by the accretion of fine sediment grains by matted colonies of cyanobacteria (formerly called blue-green algae). These were found in 3.5-billion-year-old sedimentary rocks of the Warrawoona group in a desolate place called North Pole located in Western Australia. Associated with these rocks were cherts (hard rocks composed of microscopic grains of silica) with microfilaments, which are small, threadlike structures, possibly originating from bacteria.

Figure 16 Stromatolite beds from a cliff above the Regal mine, Gila County, Arizona. Photo 1 by A. F. Shride, courtesy USGS

Figure 17   Boiling mud springs northwest of Imperial Junction, California. Photo 643 by W. C. Mendenhall, courtesy USGS

Bacteria, which descended from the earliest known form of life, still remain by far the most abundant organisms. Evidence that life began very early in the Earth's history when the planet was still quite hot exists today as thermophilic (heat-loving) bacteria, found in thermal springs and other hot-water environments (Figure 17). Because these bacteria have no nucleus, which ceases to function in hot water, they can live and reproduce successfully even at temperatures well above the normal boiling point of water as long as it remains a liquid, which requires pressures equal to those in the deep sea. The exis-

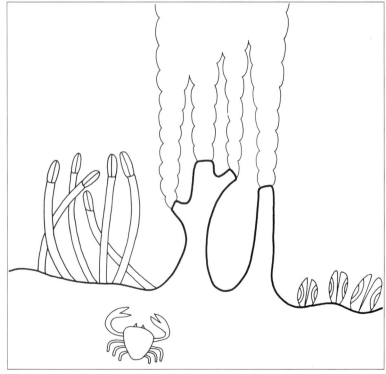

Figure 18   Tall tube worms, giant clams, and large crabs occupy the seafloor near hydrothermal vents.

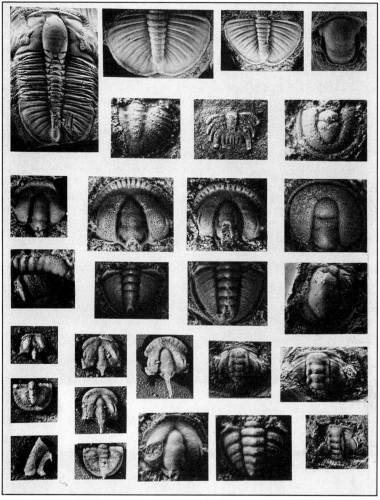

Figure 19 Trilobite fossils of the Cambrian age Carrara Formation, in the southern Great Basin of California and Nevada. Photo 47 by A. R. Palmer, courtesy USGS

tence of these organisms could be evidence that thermophiles were the common ancestors of all life on Earth.

Life probably had a very difficult time at first. When living organisms began evolving, the Earth was constantly bombarded by large meteorites. As a result, the first forms of life might have been repeatedly killed off, which forced life to regenerate over and over again. Whenever primitive organic molecules began to be arranged into living cells, the gigantic impacts would have blasted them apart before they could even reproduce. There was one safe place where life would be free to evolve, however— on the bottom of the ocean. Here, hydrothermal vents provided warmth and nourishment, and today these areas contain the most bizarre creatures the Earth has ever known (Figure 18).

Most Precambrian cherts are thought to be chemical sediments precipitated from silica-rich water in a deep ocean. The abundance of chert in the early Precambrian is evidence that most of the Earth's crust was deeply submerged in a global ocean during that time. However, cherts at the North Pole site appear to have had a shallow-water origin. This silica probably leached out of volcanic rocks that erupted into shallow seas. The silica-rich water circulated through porous sediments, dissolving the original minerals and precipitating silica in their place. Microorganisms buried in the sediments were encased in one of the hardest natural substances on Earth, and thus were able to withstand the rigors of time.

Similar cherts with microfossils of filamentous bacteria were found dating 3.4 billion years old from eastern Transvaal, South Africa. In addition, 2-billion-year-old chert from the Gunflint iron formation on the north shore of Lake Superior contained similar microfossils. These rocks were originally mined for flint to fire the flintlock rifles of the early settlers until the discovery of iron there, which made this region one of the best iron-mining districts in the country.

About 500 million years after the formation of the Gunflint chert, a new type of cell emerged in the fossil record called an eukaryote. It was characterized by a nucleus that allowed chromosomes to divide and unite hereditary material in a systematic manner. A greater number of genetic mutations were produced, providing a wide variety of organisms, some of which might have adapted to their environment better than others. These organisms were the forerunners of all the complex forms of life on Earth today.

By far, the most numerous fossils representing the first abundant life on Earth were the hard parts of marine animals lacking backbones, called invertebrates. Perhaps the best known of these creatures were the trilobites (Figure 19), which were primitive arthropods and ancestors of today's horseshoe crab. They first appeared at the base of the Paleozoic era, about 570 million years ago. The trilobites became the dominant animals of the Paleozoic, diversifying into some 10,000 species before declining and becoming extinct after some 340 million years of existence. Because they were so widespread and lived for so long, trilobite fossils have become important markers (also called guide or index fossils) for dating Paleozoic rocks.

The demise of the trilobites might be connected to the arrival of the jawed fishes. Fish were among the first vertebrates, or animals with internal skeletons. These provided more efficient muscle attachments, which gave fish much better mobility over their invertebrate counterparts. Fish constitute over

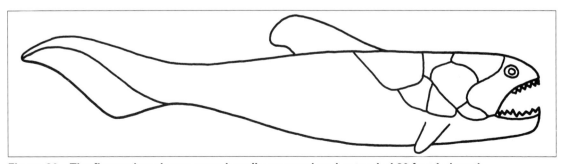

Figure 20   The fierce placoderms were heavily armored and extended 30 feet in length.

Figure 21   The emergence of plants from the sea onto the land.

half the species of verte-brates, both living and ex-tinct. The placoderms (Figure 20) were fierce giants, growing 30 feet long. They had thick armor plating around their heads that extended over and behind their jaws, which probably made them poor swimmers. They might have preyed on smaller fishes, which in turn fed on trilobites.

While fish were thriving in the ocean, plants advanced onto the land beginning some 450 million years ago (Figure 21). Within 90 million years, vast forests covered the Earth, their decay forming many of today's coal deposits (fossil fuel). Evolving along with the land plants were the arthro-pods, which constitute the largest phylum of living organisms and number roughly 1 million species, or about 80 percent of all known animals. These insects helped to pollinate the plants, whose flowers offered sweet nectar in return for services rendered. Unfortunately, because of their delicate bodies, insects did not fossilize well. However, they could be preserved if trapped in tree sap, which later hardened into amber, a clear, yellow substance that allowed the study of even the most minute body parts.

The vertebrates did not set foot on dry land until nearly 100 million years after the plants appeared. The first to come ashore were the amphibians, which evolved into reptiles, which in turn gave rise to the dinosaurs. Dinosaur bones are abundant in Jurassic and Cretaceous sediments in many parts of the country, particularly in the West. Alongside the dinosaurs evolved the mammals, which for the most part were small nocturnal creatures that fed during the night so as not to compete directly with the dinosaurs. The Cenozoic mammals are well represented in geologic his-tory. Mammoths, extinct giant mammals of the late Pleistocene Ice Age, have been well preserved in the deep freeze on top of the world.

EVIDENCE FOR EVOLUTION

During a five-year period from 1831 to 1836, the British naturalist Charles Darwin was employed as the ship's geologist aboard the HMS *Beagle* and described in great detail the rocks and fossils he encountered on his journey around the world (Figure 22). Darwin was trained as a geologist and thought like one, but today he tends to be viewed as a biologist.

Darwin observed the relationships between animals on islands and on adjacent continents as well as between animals and fossils of their extinct relatives. This study led him to conclude that species had been continuously evolving throughout time. Actually, Darwin was not the first to make this observation. Where his theory differed, however, was in postulating that new parts evolved in many tiny stages rather than in discrete jumps, which he attributed to gaps in the geologic record, caused by periods of erosion or nondeposition. Therefore, to Darwin, evolution worked at a constant tempo as species adapted to a constantly changing environment.

Darwin coined the phrase "survival of the fittest," which means that members of a species that can best utilize their environment have the best chance of producing offspring that possess the survival characteristics of their parents. In other words, successful parents have a better chance of passing on their "good" genes to their offspring, which in turn are better able to survive in their respective environment. Natural selection therefore favored those best suited to their environment at the expense of weaker species. Contemporary geologists embraced Darwin's theory, for at last a clear understanding of the changes in body forms in fossils of different ages was at hand. Thus, they were able to place geologic events in their proper sequence by studying the evolutionary changes that took place among fossils.

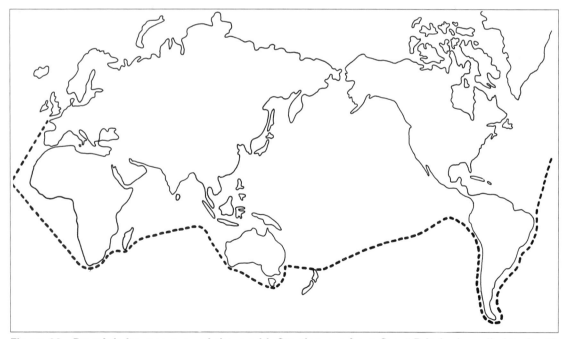

Figure 22 Darwin's journey around the world. Starting out from Great Britain, he sailed to South America, Australia, Africa, and back to Great Britain.

It now appears that evolution was not always gradual and of constant tempo as Darwin saw it. The fossil record seems to indicate that life evolved by fits and starts. There were long periods of little or no change punctuated by short periods of rapid change. Evolution might also be opportunistic, in that variations arise by chance and are selected in accordance with the demands of the environment. When the environment changes abruptly to one that is harsher, species that cannot adapt to these new conditions cannot live at their optimum and therefore cannot pass on their "bad" genes to future generations.

Gaps in the fossil record might also be the result of finding insufficient examples of intermediary species, or so-called missing links, which might have existed only in small populations. Small populations are less likely to leave a fossil record than larger ones, because the process of fossilization favors large populations. In addition, the intermediates might not have lived in the same locality as their ancestors and thus were unlikely to be preserved along with them. New species that start out in small populations might evolve rapidly as they radiate into new environments. Then as populations increase, slower evolutionary changes would take place as the species' chances of entering into the fossil record improves.

There are statistical traps in the fossil record that might suggest differences in fossil samples where no actual difference exists. In any ecologic community, a few species occur in abundance, some occur frequently, but most are rare and occur infrequently. In addition, the odds of any individual becoming fossilized after death, and thus entering the fossil record, are extremely small. No single fossil sample will contain all the rare species in an assemblage of species. If this sample were compared with another higher up the stratigraphic column, which represents a later time in geologic history, an overlapping but different set of rare species will be recorded. Species found in the lower sample but not in the upper sample might erroneously be inferred to have gone extinct. Conversely, species that appear in the upper sample but not in the lower sample, might wrongly be thought to have originated there.

It is a commonly held belief among scientists that environmental change drives evolution, not the other way around. However, in 1979, the British chemist James Lovelock turned the scientific community on its head by proposing the Gaia hypothesis, named for the Greek goddess of the Earth. He postulated that the living world is able to control to some extent its own environment and that living organisms maintain the optimal conditions for life by regulating the climate, similar to the way the human body regulates its temperature to maintain optimal metabolic efficiency. There is also a suggestion in the Gaia hypothesis that from the very beginning life followed a well-organized pattern of growth independent of chance and natural selection. It seems that living things kept pace with all the changes in the Earth over time and might have made some major changes of their own, such as converting most of the carbon dioxide in the early atmosphere and ocean into oxygen through photosynthesis.

TABLE 3   EVOLUTION OF LIFE ON EARTH

Evolution	Origin (million years)	Atmosphere
Origin of Earth	4600	Hydrogen, helium
Origin of life	3800	Nitrogen, methane, carbon dioxide
Photosynthesis	2300	Nitrogen, carbon dioxide, oxygen
Eukaryotic cells	1400	Nitrogen, carbon dioxide, oxygen
Sexual reproduction	1100	Nitrogen, oxygen, carbon dioxide
Metazoans	700	Nitrogen, oxygen
Land plants	400	Nitrogen, oxygen
Land animals	350	Nitrogen, oxygen
Mammals	200	Nitrogen, oxygen
Humans	2	Nitrogen, oxygen

Perhaps the greatest force affecting evolutionary changes was plate tectonics and the drifting of the continents. Continental motions had a wide-ranging effect on the distribution, isolation, and evolution of species. The changes in continental configuration greatly affected global temperatures, ocean currents, productivity, and many other factors of fundamental importance to life. The positioning of the continents with respect to each other and to the equator helped determine climatic conditions. When most of the land huddled near the equatorial regions (Figure 23), the climate was warm, but when lands wandered into the polar regions the climate grew cold and brought periods of glaciation.

The changing shapes of the ocean basins due to the movement of continents affects the flow of ocean currents, the width of continental margins, and, consequently, the abundance of marine habitats. When a supercontinent breaks up, more continental margins are created, the land lowers, and the sea level rises, providing a larger habitat area for marine organisms. During times of highly active continental movements, there is greater volcanic activity, especially at spreading centers, where tectonic plates are pulled apart by upwelling magma from the upper mantle. The amount of volcanism could affect the composition of the atmosphere, the rate of mountain building, the climate, and inevitably life itself.

MASS EXTINCTIONS

Practically all the species that have ever existed on Earth are extinct. As many as 4 billion species of plants and animals are believed to have lived in the geologic past, and most of these lived during the Phanerozoic, which spanned from about 600 million years ago (mya) to the present. Throughout geologic history, species have come and gone, and those presently living represent only a small fraction of all those that have previously existed. For this reason, extinctions play such an enormous role in the evolution of life. When there is a major extinction event, new species develop to fill vacated habitats.

In the Phanerozoic, there were five major mass extinctions: the Ordovician (440 mya), the Devonian (365 mya), the Permian (240 mya), the Triassic (210 mya), and the Cretaceous (65 mya). In addition, there were five or more minor mass extinctions. All extinction events seem to indicate biologic systems in extreme stress brought on by a climatic change or a

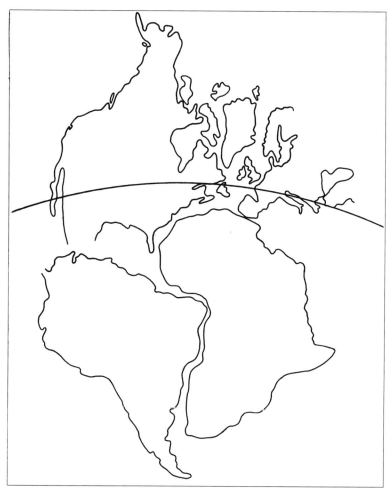

Figure 23 Approximate position of the equator during the Carboniferous period.

drop in sea level (Figure 24).

It is also speculated that extinctions are periodic, resulting from celestial influences such as cosmic rays from supernovas or by meteorite impacts. There have been 10 or more large meteorite impacts over the last 600 million years, or about one every 50 million years. Extinctions might also be episodic, with relatively long periods of stability followed by seemingly random, short-lived (geologically speaking) extinction events that only appear to be periodic. Most extinction episodes seem to select certain types of species, and analysis of the victims and the survivors might lead to the main causes of the extinctions.

Major extinction events are separated by

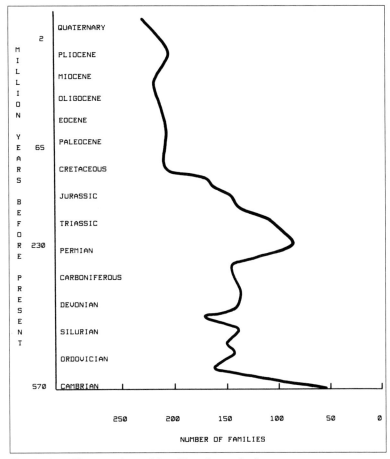

Figure 24   The number of families through time.

periods of lower extinction rates, called background extinctions, and the difference between the two is only a matter of degree. There is also a qualitative as well as a quantitative distinction between background and major extinctions. Species have regularly come and gone even during optimal conditions. Extinct species might have lost their competitive edge and were nudged out by a superior, better adapted species.

However, just because a species survived extinction does not necessarily mean it was more adaptive, but that the losers might have developed certain unfavorable traits. Therefore, it appears that those characteristics that permit a species to live successfully during normal periods for some reason become irrelevant when major extinction events occur. Thus, even though the dinosaurs became extinct, they might not have done anything "wrong" biologically.

TABLE 4   RADIATION AND EXTINCTION
OF MAJOR ORGANISMS

Organism	Radiation	Extinction
Marine invertebrates	Lower Paleozoic	Permian
Foraminiferans	Silurian	Permian & Triassic
Graptolites	Ordovician	Silurian & Devonian
Brachiopods	Ordovician	Devonian & Carboniferous
Nautiloids	Ordovician	Mississippian
Ammonoids	Devonian	Upper Cretaceous
Trilobites	Cambrian	Carboniferous & Permian
Crinoids	Ordovician	Upper Permian
Fishes	Devonian	Pennsylvanian
Land plants	Devonian	Permian
Insects	Upper Paleozoic	
Amphibians	Pennsylvania	Permian-Triassic
Reptiles	Permian	Upper Cretaceous
Mammals	Paleocene	Pleistocene

Those species that survived mass extinctions radiated outward to fill new environments, which in turn produced entirely new species. The new species might develop novel adaptations that give them a survival advantage over other species. The adaptations might lead to exotic-looking species that prosper during normal background times, but because of their overspecialization they are incapable of surviving mass extinctions. Thus, the fossil record shows a myriad of strange creatures, the likes of which have never been seen since.

The geologic record seems to imply that nature is constantly experimenting with new forms of life, and when one fails it goes extinct, and the odds that its particular combination of genes will reappear are astronomical. Thus, evolution seems to run on a one-way track, and although it perfects species to live at their optimum in their respective environments, it can never go back to the past. That is why even though in the distant future, the environment might match that of the Cretaceous period when the dinosaurs roamed the Earth, they will never return.

Because dinosaurs were not the only species to go, and because 70 percent of all known species vanished at the end of the Cretaceous, indicates that something in the environment made them all unfit to survive, yet did not significantly affect the mammals. The dinosaurs and the mammals had coexisted for more than 100 million years. After the dinosaurs became extinct, the mammals underwent an explosive evolutionary radiation, which gave rise to many unusual species. The mammals successfully replaced the dinosaurs probably because they were warm-blooded and more intelligent, which might have given them a decisive edge during times of environmental stress. The mammals also gave live birth and nurtured and protected their young, which gave them a better chance of survival. However, there is some evidence to support the belief that dinosaurs gave live birth and nurtured their young as well.

Many geologists are beginning to accept catastrophe as a normal occurrence in Earth history and, therefore, as a part of the uniformitarian process, also called gradualism. Certain periods of mass extinctions appear to be the result of some catastrophic event, such as the bombardment of one or more large asteroids or comets, rather than subtle changes, such as a change in climate or sea level or an increase in predation. Therefore, mass extinctions appear to be part of a pattern of life throughout the Phanerozoic.

GEOLOGIC AGE DATING

Geologists measure geologic time by tracing fossils through the rock strata and noticing the greater change with the deeper rocks compared to those near the surface. Fossil-bearing strata can be followed horizontally over great distances, because a particular fossil bed can be identified in another locality with respect to beds above and below it. These are called marker beds and are used for identifying geologic formations. They originally were used for the exploration of coal, one of the first practical uses of geology. Since coal-bearing seams are generally the same age and were laid down during times of abundant plant life, geologists could determine where to mine coal by studying the fossil content of the rocks.

When fossils are arranged according to their age, they do not present a random or haphazard picture, but instead show progressive changes from simple to complex forms and reveal the advancement of the species through time. Paleontologists are thus able to recognize geologic time periods based on groups of organisms that were especially plentiful and characteristic during a particular time. Within each period, there are many subdivisions determined by the occurrence of certain species, and this

Figure 25 Scientist dating a sample by the radiocarbon method.
Courtesy USGS

same succession is never out of order and is found on every major continent.

Both large and small extinctions were used by 19th-century geologists to define the boundaries of the geologic time scale. But because there was no means of actually dating rocks, the entire geologic record was delineated using relative dating techniques, which only indicated which bed was older or younger in accordance to its fossil content. Therefore, relative dating only places rocks in their proper sequence or order and does not indicate how long ago an event took place, only that it followed one event and preceded another. Before the development of radiometric dating techniques, geologists had no method of dating events precisely. So relative dating techniques were developed and are still used today. Absolute dating methods did not replace these techniques, however, but only supplemented them.

Radiocarbon dating was discovered in the late 1940s. By a comparison of carbon-14 and carbon-12 in a sample, radiocarbon dates could be determined by chemical analysis (Figure 25). The development of improved analytical techniques over the past several years has greatly increased the usefulness of radiocarbon dating, and it can now be used to date events taking place during the last ice age, which began some 100,000 years ago. This allows paleontologists, anthropologists, archaeologists, and historians to accurately date events taking place in our far past. Other radioactive elements are used to date rocks extending to the beginning of the Earth.

3

ROCK TYPES

Since all fossil remains and mineral finds are extracted from rocky beds, we will consider first how rocks are formed, and then in the following chapters discuss how fossils and minerals are deposited, shaped, located, and extracted.

A rock is a consolidated mass of Earth material and can range from a diamond, the hardest known natural substance, to ice, also considered a mineral. Generally, however, rocks are siliceous materials composed of the elements oxygen, silicon, aluminum, iron, calcium, sodium, magnesium, and potassium, which together account for over 90 percent of the Earth's crust. Oxygen is the most abundant element on Earth, constituting over 90 percent of the rocks, and the wide variety of minerals is determined by all the possible arrangements of oxygen atoms. Of the roughly 2000 known minerals, only about 20 are common, and less than half of these constitute over 90 percent of all rocks.

The three major rock groups are *igneous*, *sedimentary*, and *metamorphic*. Igneous rocks are derived directly from molten rock, or magma, which either invades the crust to form granitic rocks or erupts on the Earth's surface to produce volcanic rocks. Sedimentary rocks are cemented particles or grains that were derived from igneous, metamorphic, or other sedimentary rocks. They also precipitate directly from seawater by biologic and chemical processes. Metamorphic rocks were once igneous or sedimentary rocks that have undergone major changes due to the intense temperatures and pressures deep inside the Earth. Each of these classes contain various rock specimens with specific characteristics that make them readily identifiable.

IGNEOUS ROCKS

The first rocks to form on Earth were igneous rocks, which are derived directly from molten magma. There are two major classes of igneous rocks: intrusives, derived from the invasion of the crust by a magma body from below, and extrusives, derived from the eruption of magma onto the Earth's surface from a fissure or a volcano. Both types of rocks share much the same chemical composition but have different textures, because magma that pours out on the surface as lava tends to cool more rapidly, producing finer crystals. Intrusive bodies take much longer to cool because the rocks they invade make good insulators and tend to hold in the heat. This allows large crystals to grow, and, generally, the larger the magma body, the longer it takes to cool and, consequently, the larger the crystals.

Intrusive magma bodies come in several shapes and sizes (Figure 26). The largest are called *batholiths*, which are greater than 40 square miles and are usually longer than they are wide. Batholiths produce some of the major mountain ranges such as the Sierra Nevada in California (Figure 27), which are nearly 400 miles long and about 50 miles wide. Batholiths are composed of granitic rocks with large crystals, mostly quartz, feldspar, and mica. The rocks might contain regions where ores have accumulated in veins, which were formed when metal-rich fluids from a magma chamber migrated into cracks and fractures in the rocks. For this reason these mountains are such favorite hunting grounds for prospectors in search of gold and other valuable minerals.

An intrusive magma body smaller than 40 square miles is called a *stock*, which might be a projection of a larger batholith buried deeper down. They also are composed of coarse-grained

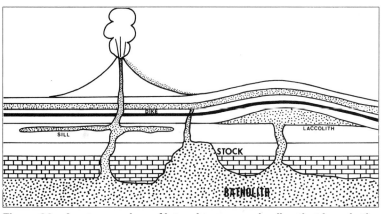

Figure 26   A cutaway view of intrusive magma bodies that invade the Earth's crust and erupt on the surface as volcanoes.

Figure 27   The Sierra Nevada Range, Inyo County, California. Photo 1116 by W. C. Mendenhall, courtesy USGS

granitic rocks. If an intrusive magma body is tabular in shape and is considerably longer (on the order of several miles) than it is wide (only a few feet), it indicates that the magma fluids occupied a large crack or fissure in the crust, thus forming a *dike*. Because dike rocks are usually harder than the surrounding material, they generally form long ridges when exposed by erosion. Large dikes can be seen radiating outward from Shiprock (Figure 28), which is a 1300-foot volcanic neck located in the northwestern corner of New Mexico.

Sills are similar to dikes in their tabular form but are produced parallel to planes of weakness such as sedimentary beds. A special type of sill is called a *laccolith*, which tends to bulge the overlying sediments upward, sometimes forming mountains like the Henry Mountains in southern Utah. Both dikes and sills are small bodies compared with batholiths and therefore cool more rapidly, providing somewhat finer grained granitic rocks.

A volcanic neck or plug is a vertical cylindrical body, ranging up to 1 mile in diameter. It is composed of solidified magma that once filled the main conduit or pipe of a volcano, and erosion has left the more resistant rock standing above the surrounding terrain. The most prominent volcanic neck in North America is Devil's Tower in northeastern Wyoming (Figure 29).

Igneous rocks are classified according to their mineral content and tex-

Figure 28   Shiprock, showing large dike, San Juan County, New Mexico. Photo 3063 by W. T. Lee, courtesy USGS

Figure 29   Devil's Tower, Crook County, Wyoming. Courtesy USGS

ture, which in turn are governed by the degree of separation and rate of cooling of the magma. The first mineral to form with falling temperatures is olivine (Figure 30), followed by pyroxene, amphibole, and biotite for the iron-magnesium silicates, known as sima (from *silica* and *magnesium*). For the aluminum silicates, known as sial (from *silica* and *aluminum*), calcium and sodium feldspar, called plagioclase, are the first minerals to form. Upon further cooling of the magma, sima and sial grade into potassium feldspar (orthoclase and microcline), followed by muscovite and finally quartz, the lowest temperature mineral to form. Texture is controlled by the rate of cooling with the slowest rate giving rise to the largest crystals and the more rapid rates providing smaller crystals, until the cooling becomes so rapid that a natural glass, called obsidian, forms.

The major igneous rocks include:

1. granite, consisting mostly of coarse-grained quartz and potassium (pink) feldspar
2. syenite, which is similar in texture to granite but with little or no quartz
3. monzonite, which has about equal proportions of plagioclase (white) feldspar and potassium feldspar with abundant dark accessory minerals
4. diorite, which resembles monzonite but with plagioclase the dominate feldspar

5. gabbro, whose chief minerals are pyroxine and plagioclase feldspar
6. peridotite, consisting principally of olivine and pyroxine
7. rhyolite, the volcanic equivalent of granite
8. andesite, the volcanic equivalent of diorite
9. basalt, the volcanic equivalent of gabbro and the most abundant of all lavas.

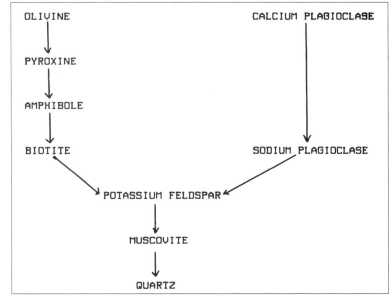

Figure 30   Sequence of mineral formation with falling temperature.

Figure 31   Eruption of Mount St. Helens on May 18, 1980. Courtesy USGS #5

If magma extrudes onto the Earth's surface either through a fissure eruption, the most prevalent kind, or a volcanic eruption, which builds majestic mountains (Figure 31), it produces a variety of rock types depending on the source material, which in turn controls the type of eruption. Ejecta from volcanoes have a wide range of chemical, mineral, and physical properties (Table 5). Nearly all volcanic products are silicate rocks, composed mainly of oxygen, silicon, and aluminum, with lesser amounts of iron, calcium, magnesium, sodium, and potassium. Basalts are relatively low in silica and high in calcium, magnesium, and iron. Magmas that have larger amounts of silica, sodium, and potassium along with lesser amounts of magnesium and iron form rhyolites, which contain mostly quartz grains, and andesites, which contain mostly feldspar grains.

TABLE 5   CLASSIFICATION OF VOLCANIC ROCKS

Property	Basalt	Andesite	Rhyolite
Silica content	Lowest about 50%, a basic rock	Intermediate about 60%	Highest more than 65%, an acid rock
Dark mineral content	Highest	Intermediate	Lowest
Typical minerals	Feldspar Pyroxene Olivine Oxides	Feldspar Amphibole Pyroxene Mica	Feldspar Quartz Mica Amphibole
Density	Highest	Intermediate	Lowest
Melting point	Highest	Intermediate	Lowest
Molten rock viscosity at the surface	Lowest	Intermediate	Highest
Formation of lavas	Highest	Intermediate	Lowest
Formation of pyroclastics	Lowest	Intermediate	Highest

All solid particles ejected into the air by volcanic eruptions are collectively called *tephra*, from the Greek word meaning "ash." (Actually, ash is a historical misnomer left over from the days when volcanoes were thought to arise from the burning of subterranean substances.) Tephra includes an assortment of fragments from dust-size material to large blocks. It results when molten rock containing volatiles, which help make magma flow easily and are composed of water and dissolved gases, mostly carbon dioxide, rises through a conduit and suddenly separates into liquid and bubbles as it nears the surface. With decreasing pressure, the bubbles grow larger. If this event occurs near the orifice, a mass of froth might spill out and flow down the sides of the volcano, forming pumice, which, due to trapped air inside glass vesicles, can actually float on water. A classic example of this phenomenon occurred during the 1883 eruption of the Indonesian volcano Krakatoa, which sent huge blocks of floating pumice into the sea and threatened shipping in the area.

If the reaction occurs deep in the throat of a volcano, the bubbles might expand explosively and burst the surrounding liquid, which fractures the magma into fragments. Like pellets from a shotgun, the fragments are driven upward by the force of the expansion and hurled high above the volcano. The fragments cool and solidify during their flight through the air. Blobs of still fluid magma called volcanic bombs might splatter the ground nearby. If they cool in flight, they form a variety of shapes, depending on how fast they are spinning, which can make them whistle as they fly through the air. If the bombs are about the size of a nut, they are called *lapilli* (Latin for "little stones") and form strange gravel-like deposits along the base of a volcano.

Lava is molten magma that reaches the throat of

Figure 32 Pahoehoe lava flow from an eruption of the Kilauea Volcano, Hawaii. Photo by D. A. Swanson, courtesy USGS

a volcano or the top of a fissure vent without exploding into fragments and is able to flow onto the surface. The magma that produces lava is much less viscous, or more fluid, than the magma that produces tephra. This allows volatiles and gases to escape more easily and gives rise to much quieter and milder eruptions. Lava is mostly composed of basalt, which contains only about 50 percent silica, dark colored, and quite fluid. The outpourings of lava come in two general classes that have Hawaiian names and are typical of Hawaiian eruptions: *pahoehoe* (pronounced pah-HOE-ay-hoe-ay), which means "satinlike," and *aa* (pronounced AH-ah), which is the sound made by someone in pain when walking over lava barefoot.

Pahoehoe, or ropy lavas (Figure 32), are highly fluid basalt flows produced when the surface of the flow congeals and forms a thin plastic skin. The melt beneath continues to flow outward, molding and remolding the skin into billowing or ropy-looking surfaces. When the lava eventually solidifies, the skin retains the appearance of the flow pressures exerted on it from below. Aa, or blocky lava, forms when viscous, subfluid lava presses forward, carrying a thick, brittle crust along with it. As the lava flows, it

Figure 33   Devil's Postpile National Monument, Madera County, California.   Photo by F. E. Mathews, courtesy USGS

stresses the overriding crust, breaking it into rough, jagged blocks, which are pushed ahead of or dragged along with the flow in a disorganized mass.

Highly fluid lava moves rapidly, especially down the steep slopes of a volcano. The speed of the flow is also determined by the viscosity of the lava and how long it takes to harden. Most lavas flow at a walking pace to about 10 miles per hour. Some lava flows have been clocked at only a snail's pace, while others move as fast as 50 miles per hour. Some very thick lavas creep ahead slowly for months or even years before they finally solidify.

After a stream of lava has crusted over and hardened on the surface and if the underlying magma continues to flow away, a long lava tube or lava cave is formed. Lava tubes can reach 10 yards across and extend for hundreds of yards. The walls and roof of a lava cave are occasionally adorned with stalactites that grow from the ceiling, and the floor is covered with stalagmites that grow from the bottom up, composed of deposits of lava. In some cases, especially on the ocean floor, the lava solidifies into pillow-shaped masses called pillow lava. As a lava flow cools, it shrinks, causing cracking or jointing. The cracks can shoot vertically through the entire lava flow, breaking it into six-sided pillars or columns like those found at Devils Postpile National Monument in east-central California (Figure 33).

Sedimentary Rocks

Sedimentary rocks are derived from the weathering or decomposition of older rocks, including igneous, metamorphic, and other sedimentary rocks. There are two basic classes of sedimentary rocks: *clastics*, comprising particles or grains, and *precipitates*, comprising water-dissolved minerals, mostly calcium and silica. In addition, dissolved minerals in groundwater can cement clastic particles together to form solid rock beneath the Earth's surface.

Rocks are weathered, or broken down, into sediment grains by the action of wind, water, cycles of heating and freezing, and the activities of plants and animals. Weathering causes rocks to break apart or the outer layers to peal or spall off in a process known as exfoliation. The products of weathering include a range of materials from very-fine-grained sediments to large boulders. Erosion by wind, rain, or glacial ice eventually brings the sediments to streams and rivers, which in turn empty into the ocean. The more angular the sediment grains, the less time they have spent in transit, whereas the more rounded sediment grains indicate severe abrasion from long-distance travel or reworking by fast-flowing streams or pounding waves.

When the suspended sediments reach the ocean, they settle out under the influence of gravity according to grain size, with the coarser-grained

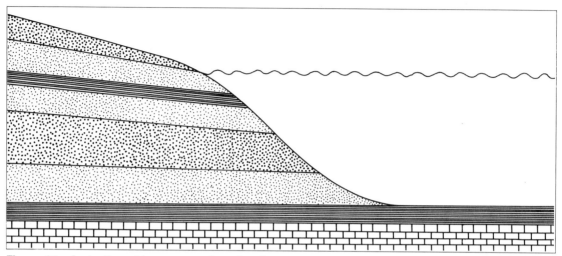

Figure 34 A stratigraphic cross section showing a sequence of sandstones, siltstones, and shales overlying a basement rock composed of limestone.

sediments settling out near the turbulent shore and the finer-grained sediments settling out in calmer waters farther out to sea. As the shoreline advances toward the sea due to the buildup of coastal sediments or falling sea levels, finer sediments are progressively covered over by coarser ones. As the shoreline recedes due to rising sea levels, coarser sediments are covered over by progressively finer ones. This provides a reoccurring sequence of sandstones, siltstones, and shales (Figure 34).

Terrestrial sediments are formed entirely on land and include deposits of windblown sand, called eolian deposits, which are identified by sand dunes; river deposits, identified by cross-bedding and ripple marks; lake or marsh deposits, which can contain fossils and coal beds; and glacial deposits, which are distinctive heaped sediments deposited in place, where the glaciers melted.

Sand moves across the desert floor by a process known as saltation (Figure 35). When a windblown sand grain lands, its momentum kicks up another sand grain, which, when it falls, kicks up another in a sort of chain reaction. This forms sand dunes that march across the desert floor in the direction of the prevailing wind, engulfing everything in their paths. The process can be particularly troublesome for regions bordering deserts such as the Sahel region south of the Sahara Desert in Africa. Desertification is becoming a serious problem throughout many parts of the world, turning once fertile agricultural land into desert by the destructive activities of humans and Nature.

Clastic sedimentary rocks are generally classified according to grain size. Gravel-size sediments are called conglomerates if they are rounded and breccia if they are angular. They are composed of abundant quartz and chalcedony (microcrystalline quartz, i.e., flint or chert). Glacial deposits composed of boulders and gravel-size sediments are called moraines or tillites. Sandstones are composed of mostly quartz grains roughly the size of beach sands. Indeed, many sandstones such as the St. Peter sandstone of the central United States, which is used for the manufacture of glass, were once beach deposits. If a sandstone has abundant feldspar as well as quartz, it is called an arkose. Siltstones are composed of fine quartz grains that are still visible to the naked eye. Shales or mudstones are composed of the finest sedimentary particles in clay or mud, whose grains are invisible to the unaided eye.

Clastic sediments are lithified, or turned into rock, mainly by compaction for fine-grained sediments and cementation for coarse-grained, well-sorted sediments, which have grains of equal size. As increasing layers of sediments pile up, water is squeezed out of the lower strata by the overlying weight until individual grains are pressed together. Older sediments might show a higher degree of compaction because they were buried more deeply, although the degree of compaction is not always a reliable indicator of age.

Minerals such as calcium carbonate and silica are dissolved in groundwater, which flows around coarse sediment grains. The minerals are deposited between sediment grains and cement them together. If iron oxides are the cementing agents, they tend to color the rocks red, brown, or yellow. Such colors typify terrestrial sediments. If clays are used as cementing agents for poorly sorted marine sediments, which have grains of varying sizes, they tend to color the rock gray or gray-green.

Nonclastic, or precipitate, rocks such as limestones are formed by biologic and chemical precipitation of minerals dissolved in water. Rainwater normally has a small amount of carbonic acid (the same acid in soft drinks) from the chemical reaction of water and carbon dioxide in the atmosphere. This acid plays an important role in dissolving calcium and silica minerals from surface rocks to form bicarbonates. The bicarbonates enter rivers that

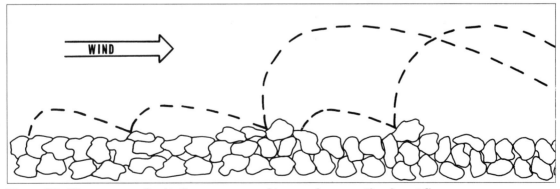

Figure 35   The process of saltation causes sand to march across the desert floor.

reach the ocean and become thoroughly mixed with seawater by the action of waves and currents.

The bicarbonates precipitate mostly by biologic activity as well as direct chemical processes. Living organisms require calcium bicarbonate to build supporting structures such as shells composed of calcium carbonate. When the organism dies, its skeleton falls to the ocean floor, where over time, thick deposits of calcium carbonate called calcite ooze build up to form limestone (Figure 36). If the ocean is deeper than about 2 miles, a depth called the calcium carbonate compensation zone, the calcium carbonate remains are dissolved in the cold waters of the abyssal.

Limestone is the most common precipitate rock and is mostly produced by biologic activity. This is evidenced by the abundance of fossils of marine life in limestone beds. If limestone is composed almost entirely of fossils or their fragments, it is called a coquina. Some limestone is chemically precipitated directly from seawater, and a minor amount precipitates in evaporite deposits from brines. Chalk is a soft, porous carbonate rock, and one of the largest chalk deposits is the chalk cliffs of Dorset, England, which, because they are soft, severely erode during violent coastal storms. Dolomite, which resembles limestone, is produced by the replacement of calcium in limestone with magnesium. The replacement can cause a reduction in volume, forming void spaces, which can destroy any fossils that are present.

Silica also dissolves in seawater in volcanically active areas on the seafloor, from volcanic eruptions into the sea, and from weathering of siliceous rocks on the continents. Some organisms like diatoms (Figure 37) extract the dissolved silica directly from seawater to make their shells or skeletons. Accumulations of siliceous sediment on the ocean floor from dead organisms form diatomaceous earth, also called diatomite. If this is lithified into solid rock, it forms chalcedony, which also forms by direct precipitation from seawater. Chalcedony produces varieties of opal (which can recrystallize into chert), banded agate, jasper, and flint.

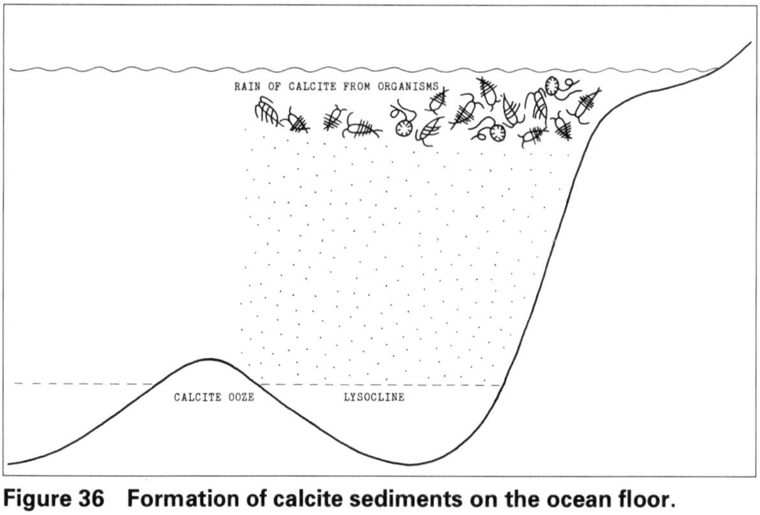

Evaporite deposits are produced in arid regions near shore, where pools of brine, which are constantly replenished with seawater, evaporate in the hot sun, leaving salts behind. The salts precip-

Figure 36 Formation of calcite sediments on the ocean floor.

itate out of solution in stages. The first mineral to precipitate is calcite, closely followed by dolomite, although only a small amount of limestone and dolostone is produced in this manner. After about two-thirds of the water is evaporated, gypsum precipitates. When nine-tenths of the water is removed, halite, or common salt, forms. Thick deposits of halite are also produced by the direct precipitation of seawater in deep basins that have been cut off from the general circulation of the ocean such as the Mediterranean Sea and the Red Sea.

Coal is generally regarded as a sedimentary rock, even though it did not originate from clastic sediments or from chemical precipitation. Instead, coal originated from compacted plant life that grew in lush swamps. Often between easily separated layers of

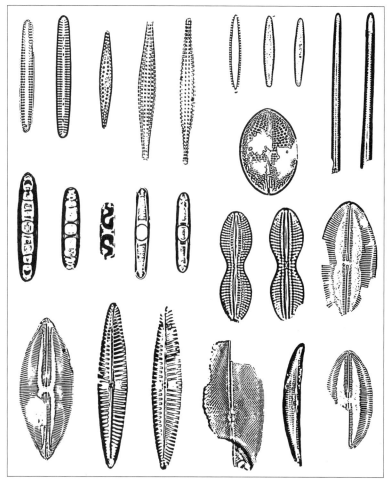

Figure 37   Miocene marine diatoms from the Choptank formation, Calvert County, Maryland. Photo by G. W. Andrews, courtesy USGS

coal or associated fine-grained sedimentary beds are carbonized remains of ancient plant stems and leaves. Black or carbonized shales also originated in the ancient coal swamps, and traces of plant life can be found between shale layers.

METAMORPHIC ROCKS

Igneous and sedimentary rocks that have been subjected to the intense temperatures and pressures of the Earth's interior, by heat generated near magma bodies, by shear pressures from Earth movements, or by strong chemical reactions that do not cause the rocks to melt are called metamorphic rocks, so named because of the material changes that have taken place within the rocks themselves. Metamorphism causes dramatic changes in texture, mineral composition, or both, so that it is often difficult to determine the nature of the original rock.

TABLE 6 CLASSIFICATION OF ROCKS

Group	Characteristics	Environment
Igneous		
Intrusives	Granite. Mostly quartz and potassium feldspar with mica, pyroxene, and amphibole.	Deep-seated coarse-grained pluton
	Syenite. Mostly potassium feldspar with mica, pyroxine, and amphibole.	Deep-seated medium-grained pluton
	Monzonite. Plagioclase and potassium feldspar with mica, pyroxine, and amphibole.	Deep-seated coarse-grained pluton
	Diorite. Mostly plagioclase and quartz with abundant mica, pyroxine, and amphibole.	Deep-seated coarse-grained pluton
	Gabbro. Equal amounts of plagioclase and mica, pyroxine, and amphibole.	Intermediate depth medium- to coarse-grained pluton
	Peridotite. Mostly olivine, pyroxine, and amphibole with little plagioclase.	Very-deep-seated medium- to fine-grained pluton
Extrusives	Rhyolite. Mostly quartz and potassium feldspar with mica, pyroxene, and amphibole.	Fine-grained fissue or volcanic eruption

ROCK TYPES

Group	Characteristics	Environment
	Andesite. Mostly pla- gioclase and quartz with abundant mica, pyroxine, and amphi- bole.	Fine-grained fissure or volcanic eruption
	Basalt. Equal amounts of plagioclase and mica, pyroxine, and am- phibole.	Fine-grained fissure or volcanic eruption
Sedimentary		
Clastic	Conglomerate. Frag- ments of rounded gravel-size sediments.	River and glacial deposits
	Breccia. Fragments of angular gravel-size sed- iments.	River and volcanic deposits
	Sandstone. Coarse- grained quartz and feld- spar with minor accessory minerals.	Marine and river deposits
	Siltstone. Fine-grained quartz and feldspar with minor accessory minerals.	Marine, lake, and river deposits
	Shale. Very-fine- grained sediments, mostly feldspar.	Marine and lake deposits
Nonclastic	Limestone. Calcium car- bonate often with skele- tal fragments.	Marine and lake deposits
	Dolomite. Calcium magnesium carbonate.	Marine deposits and veins
	Gypsum. Hydrous cal- cium sulfate.	Near shore brine pools
	Chalcedony. Micro- scopic silica.	Deep marine and groundwater

Group	Characteristics	Environment
Metamorphic		
Foliated	Gneiss. Mostly quartz and feldspar with mica and amphibole.	Coarse grained, deep seated
	Schist. Mostly mica and platy minerals with less quartz and feldspar.	Coarse grained, deep seated
	Phyllite. Micaceous rock intermediate between schist and slate.	Medium grained, moderate depth
	Slate. Feldspar, quartz, and micaceous minerals.	Fine grained, moderate depth
Nonfoliated	Hornfels. Metamorphic clay material.	Contact with hot magma bodies
	Marble. Metamorphic carbonates.	Coarse grained, deep seated
	Quartzite. Metamorphic sandstone.	Fine grained, deep seated

Metamorphism produces new textures by recrystallization, whereby minerals grow into larger crystals, which might have a different orientation. The crystals grow by laying down layers upon layers of atoms (see Chapter 7 on crystals). New minerals are also created by recombining chemical elements to form new associations. Water and gasses from nearby magma bodies also aid in the chemical changes taking place in rocks by conveying chemical elements from one place to another.

Although there are many minerals that are strictly metamorphic in origin, most metamorphic rocks are similar in composition to their parent rocks. Heat is probably the most important agent for recrystallization, and often deep burial is required to generate the temperatures and pressures required for extensive metamorphism. Varying degrees of metamorphism are also achieved at shallower depths in geologically active areas with higher thermal gradients, where the temperature increases with depth much greater than normal.

During metamorphism, rocks behave plastically and are able to bend or stretch due to the high temperatures and the great pressures applied by the overlying rocks. The stress might deform the rocks and flatten or stretch

Figure 38   Precambrian Vishnu Schist, Grand Canyon National Park, Arizona. Photo 52 by R. M. Turner, courtesy USGS

pebbles or fossils. Generally, most fossils are destroyed during intense or prolonged metamorphism as the rocks recrystallize under stress, erasing all evidence of fossils.

Because any rock type can be metamorphosed, there is a wide range of metamorphic rocks, but basically they can be classified into two major categories: *foliated*, with a layered or banded structure, and *nonfoliated*, with a massive structure. Mountain building, which provides the forces necessary for folding and faulting rocks at shallow depths, also provides the stress forces need to produce foliated metamorphic rocks deeper down. The most common foliated metamorphosed rocks are called schist and gneiss (pronounced like nice).

A schist is an intensely foliated crystalline rock with much mica and little feldspar, which causes it to readily split along layers. A spectacular crystalline schist called Vishnu Schist lies on the bottom of the western end of the Grand Canyon (Figure 38). A gneiss is a metamorphic equivalent of granite with abundant feldspar. It is the most coarsely banded metamorphic rock, consisting of alternating bands. The lighter bands are rich in quartz and feldspar, and the darker bands are rich in biotite mica, hornblende, or garnet.

Low-grade metamorphism transforms shale into slate, a uniformly fine-grained rock that splits easily into smooth slabs, which makes it useful for such things as chalkboards and building materials. The metamorphism causes a mechanical reorientation of clay particles as well as minor recrystallization. Slate is often colored black from carbon that has been metamorphosed into graphite. Iron minerals give slate a red color, and magnesium minerals give it a green color. Intermediate in texture between a schist and slate is phyllite, which tends to break into slabs with a slightly wrinkled surface.

Nonfoliated rocks consist of hornfels, which formed by contact metamorphism in narrow belts around intrusive magma bodies (Figure 39). Their formation is similar to the baking of clay in a kiln to make pottery. This produces fine-grained, hard rocks that can be either completely recrystallized with none of the original features preserved or only slightly modified with most of the original features kept intact.

Single mineral crystalline metamorphic rocks are produced from limestone or sandstone. Marble is the product of the metamorphism of limestone or dolomite, but is distinguishable from limestone by its larger crystals and sometimes spectacular fossils on a polished surface. Quartzite is produced by the metamorphism of sandstone. Its sugary luster distinguishes quartzite from chalcedony, which has a nearly waxlike luster.

A special kind of metamorphism results when rocks are broken, sheared, shocked, or ground on or near the Earth's surface, where temperatures and

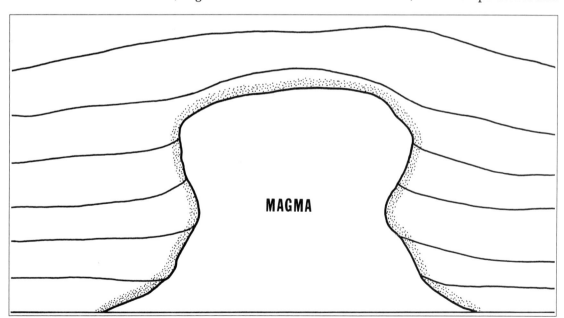

Figure 39 Contact metamorphism is produced by the intrusion of a magma body into overlying rocks, as shown here.

pressures are too low to cause significant recrystallization. When a fault slips, it produces a tremendous amount of pressure and frictional heat at the point of contact between fault planes in a very short time. This produces a metamorphic rock that results from grinding or milling by the fault movement and is similar to a schist.

Meteorite impact craters are surrounded by circular disturbed areas, consisting of rocks that have been reworked by shock metamorphism. Large meteorite impacts gouge out tremendous amounts of Earth material and send it high into the atmosphere, where it can shade the planet and produce substantial climatic changes that cause biologic havoc. Five such impact craters have been discovered, dating back to around the time when the dinosaurs became extinct.

4

FOSSIL FORMATION

M ost of the Earth's surface is covered by a thin veneer of sediment. Under special geologic conditions, and with no predation or decomposition and rapid burial, the bodies of dead organisms are preserved to withstand the rigors of time. Most fossils are comprised of ancient marine organisms because they are the oldest form of animal life and were the most abundant, and therefore stood a better chance of becoming fossilized. The ocean, where sedimentation occurs, also provided the ideal setting for the preservation of species.

However, some organisms, especially those with soft bodies, are not as well preserved in the fossil record. Thus, fossils are dominated by organisms with hard skeletal remains, and shells, bones, teeth, and wood dominate the record of past life. Unfortunately, because preservation must meet these conditions, the fossil record is well represented by organisms with hard body parts but poorly represented, or not represented at all, by organisms with soft body parts. This gives the fossil record a somewhat lopsided view of previous life on Earth.

THE FOSSIL FAMILY TREE

Fossils of extinct organisms are classified by the same system used for classifying living organisms. The first classification scheme was developed by the 18th-century Swedish botanist Carolus Linnaeus, who gave Latin names to organisms because Latin was the universal language of science during his time. His naming was based on the number of characteristics organisms had in common, for instance birds, bats, and pterosaurs all had wings.

Linnaeus realized that some organisms had a greater similarity than others because they were more closely related. Later, as evolution was recognized as the process by which organisms develop into new species, classification schemes were developed to describe these evolutionary patterns, demonstrating how groups of organisms were related in both space and time.

In the classification scheme used by biologists and paleontologists, each organism is assigned an italicized, two-part species name. The first word, which is capitalized, is the generic name and is shared with other very closely related species. The second word, written in lowercase, is the species name and is unique to a particular genus: for example, *Homo sapiens*—which is us.

Often the name of the discoverer of a new species and the date of discovery will follow the species name. The scientific name of a species is written in a Grecian or a Latinized form to provide enough names to go around since there are well over 2 million known species. Every species must have a unique name, and that name cannot be used again for another species; neither can more than one name be applied to the same species.

TABLE 7   CLASSIFICATION OF ORGANISM

Kingdom

    Phylum

        Class

            Order

                Family

                    Genus

                        Species

The classification scheme establishes a hierarchy (Table 7) in which each step up the ladder becomes more inclusive, encompassing a larger number of organisms. A kingdom comprises all the species of either animals, plants, or microorganisms. The kingdom we belong to is Animalae; our phylum is Chordata; our subphylum is Vertebrata; our class is Mammalia;

Figure 40 *Homo erectus* **on the hunt.** Courtesy National Museums of Canada

our order is Primate; and our family is Hominidea. Genus and species are the lowest rungs of the classification hierarchy. Our genus *Homo* encompasses all our ancient ancestors (Figure 40), starting with *Homo habilis*, who lived around 2 million years ago.

The vast majority of fossils found are those of marine animals. More remains of marine organisms have been preserved because seawater is a good preservative and sedimentation takes place more readily in water. In addition, marine life has been around about eight times longer than terrestrial life; therefore, there were a greater number of organisms available for fossilization.

The vast majority of marine fossils are included in 10 phyla. The first phylum, Protozoa, begins with the simplest life forms, and each succeeding phylum—Porifera, Coelenterata, Bryozoa, Brachipoda, Mollusca, Annelida, Arthropoda, and Echinodermata—becomes more complex, with the phylum Chordata, where we belong, the most complex of all. The ordering of phyla in this manner is in recognition of the evolutionary advancement of species (Table 8).

TABLE 8   CLASSIFICATION OF FOSSILS

Group	Characteristics	Geologic Age
Protozoans	Single-celled animals. Forams and radiolarians.	Precambrian to recent
Porifera	The sponges. About 3000 living species.	Proterozoic to recent
Coelenterates	Tissues composed of three layers of cells. About 10,000 living species. Jellyfish, hydra, coral.	Cambrian to recent
Bryozoans	Moss animals. About 3000 living species.	Ordovician to recent
Brachiopods	Two asymmetrical shells. About 120 living species.	Cambrian to recent
Mollusks	Straight, curled, or two symmetrical shells. About 70,000 living species. Snails, clams, squids, ammonites.	Cambrian to recent
Annelids	Segmented body with well-developed internal organs. About 7000 living species. Worms and leaches.	Cambrian to recent
Arthropods	Largest phylum of living species with over one million known. Insects, spiders, shrimp, lobsters, crabs, trilobites.	Cambrian to recent
Echinoderms	Bottom dwellers with radial symmetry. About 5000 living species. Starfish, sea cucumbers, sand dollars, crinoids.	Cambrian to recent

Group	Characteristics	Geologic Age
Vertebrates	Spinal column and internal skeleton. About 70,000 living species. Fish, amphibians, reptiles, birds, mammals.	Ordovician to recent

The first organisms to develop on Earth were probably bacteria and ancestral blue-green algae. These were possibly fossilized into algal mats, stromatolites, and microfilaments in chert. The next stage up the evolutionary scale were the protozoans, including the amoeba, the forams, and the radiolarians, which probably built the first limestone formations.

The next step are the sponges, which belong to the phylum Porifera. Generally, the sponges did not fossilize well except for the siliceous spicules that made up their skeletons. The coelenterates include the jellyfish, sea anemones, hydra, and coral. The soft-bodied animals did not fossilize well, but the calcareous coral made excellent fossils (Figure 41) and built impressive formations of limestone. More recent corals are responsible for the construction of barrier reefs and atolls, and they even rival humans in changing the face of the Earth.

The bryozoans, or moss animals, were attached to the seafloor and filter-fed on microscopic organisms. They are important marker fossils for correlating rock formations. The brachiopods, or lamp shells, are among the most common fossils, with over 30,000 species catalogued from the fossil record. They are generally what people think of when the word fossil is mentioned. (The ancients may have found these shells on mountaintops and wondered how they got there.)

The mollusks, which include snails, clams, and squids, probably left the most important fossil record of all. The extinct ammonoids left giant fossil spiral shells, several feet in diameter. The annelids are worms and leaches, and because of their soft bodies they did not leave many fossils. However, they did leave a profusion of tracks and borings that were fairly well preserved (Figure 42). The largest phylum of living organisms is Arthropoda, which includes insects, spiders, shrimp, lobsters, and barnacles. Perhaps one of the first and best known were the extinct trilobites, whose fossils make prized possessions.

The echinoderms were possibly the strangest animals ever preserved in the fossil record. They are unique among animals by having radial symmetry with body parts radiating from a central point, a water vascular system for feeding and locomotion, and no head. Included are the sea lilies, sea cucumbers, starfish, brittle stars, and sea urchins. Fossils of ancient crinoids and blastoids are eagerly sought after by fossil hunters.

The higher animals are the chordates, which include fish, amphibians, reptiles, birds and mammals, including humans. The vertebrates were the first advanced animals to populate the land. Dinosaur bones have intrigued scientists since their first discovery in Great Britain in the early 19th century. Today, their popularity is apparent by the large numbers of visitors to natural history museums and of serious patrons of paleontology, who volunteer their time to help excavate dinosaur bones.

THE SEDIMENTARY ENVIRONMENT

Most sedimentary rocks that were deposited in the ocean contain the fossils that record much of the Earth's history. Be-

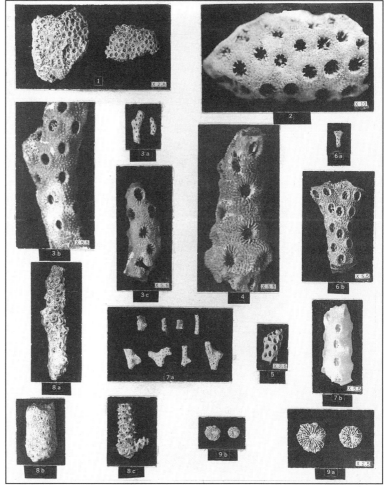

Figure 41 Fossil corals from Bikini Atoll, Marshall Islands. Photo 56 by J. W. Wells, courtesy USGS

cause the majority of marine sediments consist of material washed off the continents, most sedimentary rocks form along continental margins or in the basins of inland seas, such as the sea that invaded the interior of North America during the Jurassic and Cretaceous periods. High sediment rates form deposits up to hundreds or even thousands of feet thick. In many places, individual sedimentary beds can be traced for hundreds of miles.

The process of formation of sedimentary rock begins with erosion. Rain plays a significant role in causing erosion, as do wind and glacial ice. Raindrops impart kinetic energy to the soil when they land, kicking up sediment grains and redistributing them farther down slope. Rainwater that does not infiltrate into the ground runs off elevated areas, carrying sediment along with it. Rivulets carry sediment to streams, which transport it to rivers, which in turn dump it into the ocean. Rivers, for example, the Mississippi, carry an enormous amount of sediment that, when deposited into the Gulf of Mexico, contributes to the continuous outward building of the Gulf Coast region.

Every year, the continents receive about 25,000 cubic miles of rainwater, of which almost half runs back into the sea. An estimated 25 billion tons of sediment, much of which is from soil erosion (Figure 43), is carried by runoff into the ocean, where it settles out on the continental shelf. The continental shelf extends up to 100 miles or more and reaches a depth of roughly 600 feet. In most places, the continental shelf is nearly flat with an average slope of only about 10 feet per mile.

By comparison, the continental slope extends to an average depth of 2 miles or more and has a very steep angle of 2 to 6 degrees, comparable to the slopes of many mountain ranges. Sediments that reach the edge of the continental shelf slide down the continental slope under the influence of gravity. Often, huge masses of sediment cascade down the continental slope by gravity slides, which have been known to bury transcontinental telegraph cables under thick deposits of rubble.

Loose sediment grains are also carried by the wind, especially in dry regions, where dust storms are prevalent. The finer particles can remain suspended in the air for long periods. The sediment load in the lower atmosphere is as much as 150,000 tons per cubic mile of air. Particularly strong dust storms like those in the African Sahara Desert can transport fine-grained sediment over vast distances, even across the Atlantic Ocean to South America.

Fine sediments that land in the ocean slowly build up deposits of abyssal red clay, whose color signifies its terrestrial origin. But most of the windblown sediments remain on the land, where they form thick layers of loess, a fine-grained,

Figure 42   Fossil worm borings in the Heiser Sandstone, Pensacola Mountains, Antarctica. Photo 3 by D. L. Schmidt, courtesy USGS

sheetlike deposit. Along with these are dune deposits, composed of desert sands, which when lithified show a distinct dune structure on outcrops, consisting of cross-stratification of sand layers. In addition, the sediment grains of desert deposits are frosted, and larger rocks show a desert varnish caused by wind abrasion, similar to sandblasting, and deposits of mineral solutions exuded from within the rock.

Fluvial, or river, deposits are terrestrial sediments that remain, for the most part, on the continent after erosion. When rivers become clogged with sediments and fill their channels, they spill over onto the adjacent land and carve out a new river coarse. Thus, rivers meander their way downstream, forming thick sediment deposits in broad flood plains that can fill an entire valley. Flood waters rapidly flowing out of dry mountain regions carry a heavy sediment load, including blocks the size of automobiles. When the stream reaches the desert, its water rapidly percolates into the desert floor, and sometimes huge monoliths dot the landscape, as monuments to the tremendous power of water in motion.

Fluvial deposits are recognized in outcrops by their coarse sediment grains and cross-bedding features (Figure 44), which were produced when the stream meandered back and forth over old river channels. River currents can also align mineral grains and fossils, giving rocks a linear structure that can be used to determine the direction of current flow. Ripple marks on exposed surfaces can be used as well for determining the direction of flow, which is perpendicular to the crest line and toward the angle of least slope (Figure 45), as in present-day streams.

Much of the upper midwestern and northeastern parts of the United States were once covered by thick glaciers during the last ice age. Many areas were eroded to the granite bedrock, erasing the entire geologic history of the region. The power of glacial erosion is well demonstrated by the deep-sided valleys carved out of mountain slopes (Figure 46) by thick sheets of ice. The

Figure 43   Severe soil erosion on a farm in Shelby County, Tennessee.
Photo by Tim McCabe, courtesy USDA Soil Conservation Service

Figure 44 Close view of cross-bedding in the coarse sands of the Glenns Ferry formation, in Elmore County, Idaho. Photo 271 by H. E. Malde, courtesy USGS

glacially derived sediments covered much of the landscape, burying older rocks under thick layers of till.

Lacustrine, or lake environment, deposits are stratified similar to marine deposits only on a smaller scale, depending on the size of the lake. Glacial lakes, like the Great Lakes, which were huge pits carved out by the glaciers and later filled with meltwater, receive large amounts of sediments derived from the continent. The buildup of sediments continually make the lakes shallower until sometime in the future they will dry out completely and become flat, featureless planes.

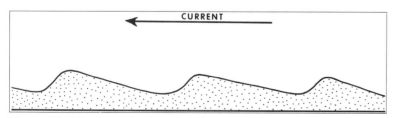

Figure 45 Ripple marks showing river current direction.

Many large lakes or inland seas in the interiors of the continents are saltwater lakes similar to the Great Salt Lake in Utah. Some salt lakes might have originated as pinched-off sections of retreating seas that once invaded the continent. Because they generally have no outlet, the lakes become saltier as rivers continue to carry salts into them. The Great Salt Lake is eight times saltier than the ocean, which gives swimmers a much better buoyancy. The Dead Sea on the border between Israel and Jordan became so salty that it completely overturned, killing off most plant and animal life.

FOSSIL PRESERVATION

Figure 46 Glacial valley and lake in the Rocky Mountains. Courtesy National Park Service

Generally, in order to be preserved in the fossil record, organisms must possess hard body parts such as shells or bones. Soft fleshy structures are quickly destroyed by predators or decayed by bacteria. Even hard parts left on the surface for any length of time will be destroyed. Therefore, organisms must be buried rapidly to escape destruction by the elements and to be protected against agents of weathering and erosion. Marine organisms thus are better candidates for fossilization than those living on the land because the ocean is typically the site of sedimentation, whereas the land is largely the site of erosion.

The beds of ancient lakes were also excellent sites for rapid burial of skeletal remains of freshwater organisms and skeletons of other animals, including those of early humans. Ancient swamps were particularly plentiful with prolific growths of vegetation, which fossilized in abundance. Many animals became trapped in bogs overgrown by vegetation. The normally reducing environment of the swamps kept bacterial decay to a minimum, which greatly aided in the preservation of plants and animals. The rapidly accumulating sediments in flood plains, deltas, and stream channels buried freshwater organisms, along with other plants and animals that happen to fall into the water.

Only a small fraction of all the organisms that have ever lived are preserved as fossils. Normally, the remains of a plant or animal are completely destroyed through predation and decay. Although it seems that fossilization is common for some organisms, for others it is almost impossible. For the most part, the remains of organisms are recycled in the Earth, which is fortunate because soil and water would soon become depleted of essential nutrients. Also, most of the fossils exposed on the Earth's surface are destroyed by weathering processes. This makes for an incomplete fossil record with poor or no representation of certain species.

The best fossils are those composed of unaltered remains. The more durable parts of some organisms, as old as 70 million years or more, have been preserved in their original composition and appearance. Generally, it is the inorganic hard parts, composed mostly of calcium carbonate, that form the vast majority of unaltered fossils. Calcite and aragonite also contribute to a substantial number of fossils of certain organisms. To a lesser extent, calcium phosphate, which constitutes the bones and teeth of most vertebrates, survives unaltered. In addition, entire bodies might be sealed in a protective medium such as tree sap, tar, or glacial ice.

The next best fossils are composed of altered remains. The original substance, whether wood or bone, is replaced by minerals from circulating solutions, or pore spaces are filled with minerals and the specimen is literally turned to stone. The most common petrifying agents carried by the groundwater are calcite and silica. If iron sulfide is used, the original material is replaced with pyrite crystals, providing a beautiful and unique specimen. The most common petrified fossils are large dinosaur bones, which can be quite heavy, and tree trunks such as those found in the Petrified Forest of Arizona (Figure 47).

If groundwater dissolves the remains buried in the sediment, a mold is left behind. The mold faithfully reflects the shape and surface markings of the organism; however, it does not reveal any information about its internal structure. When the mold is subsequently filled with mineral matter, a cast is formed (Figure 48). The brain size of fossil ani-

Figure 47   Petrified logs at the Petrified Forest National Park, Apache County, Arizona. Photo by Richard Frear, courtesy National Park Service

mals can be determined by measuring the volume of casts, called endocasts, made from the animal's skull and are exact replicas of the cranial cavity.

Leaves and delicate animal forms are preserved by carbonization. This occurs when fine sediment, such as clay, encases the remains of an organism. As time passes, pressure from overlying rocks squeezes out the liquid and gaseous components and leaves behind a thin film of carbon. Black shales deposited as organic-rich mud in oxygen-poor environments such as swamps often contain abundant carbonized remains. If the carbon film is lost from a fossil preserved in fine-grained sediment, a replica of the surface of the plant or animal, called an impression, might still show considerable detail.

Other delicate organisms, such as insects, are difficult to preserve in this manner. Consequently, they are quite rare in the fossil record. Not only do they need to be protected from decay, but they must be protected from any pressure that could crush them. Insects and even small frogs may be preserved in amber, the hardened resin or sap of ancient trees. The animal first becomes trapped in the sticky resin, which seals it off from the atmosphere and protects its remains from damaging air and water. When the resin hardens, it forms a protective, pressure-resistant case around the insect. Air is also sometimes trapped in amber. Analysis of air trapped inside Cretaceous-age amber of about 80 million years old indicates that the atmosphere might have had a much higher oxygen content than it does today, perhaps accounting in part for the giantism of the dinosaurs.

TRACKS, TRAILS, AND FOOTPRINTS

The bones of extinct animals are much rarer than their footprints, and many animals are known only by their tracks. The formation of clear foot impressions requires a moist, fine-grained, and cohesive sediment bed for the animal to walk on. If the animal walks slowly, it will leave a detailed impression of its feet. Even clear outlines of claws or nails, the shape of the footpad, and the pattern of scales can be discerned.

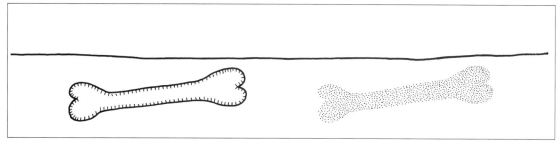

Figure 48   Comparative views of a mold (left) and a cast (right).

Unfortunately, few such high-quality fossil footprints are found, and most are partially destroyed during the sedimentary process that buries and preserves them. The most favorable conditions for the preservation of footprints exist after high-tide waters have receded, and the tracks are allowed to dry and harden and eventually fill with a different type of sediment. The weight of the animal is also important, and large animals, such as dinosaurs, leave deeper tracks that are less readily destroyed and most likely preserved.

Animal tracks tell of the earliest invasion on dry land some 370 million years ago. Primitive Devonian fish, similar to today's lungfish, crawled on their bellies from one pool to another, using lobed fins to push themselves along. The lobed-finned fish that first ventured on land gave rise to the four-legged amphibians, and their tracks are found in formations of late Devonian age. The amphibian tracks are generally broad and have a short stride, indicating that the animal could barely hold its squat body off the ground. It walked with a clumsy gait, and running was out of the question. Amphibian footprints became abundant in the Carboniferous period but less abundant in the Permian, owing to the takeover by the reptiles and due to the amphibian's preference for life in the water.

The increase of the number of reptilian footprints in the Carboniferous and the Permian plainly shows the rise of the reptiles at the expense of the amphibians. Possibly one of the major factors leading to the superiority of the reptiles was their more efficient mode of locomotion. The reptiles were also much more suited for living full-time on dry land, whereas the amphibians had to return to the water to keep their skin from drying out and for reproduction. Although most reptiles walked or ran on all fours, by the late Permian some smaller reptiles reared up on their hind legs when they wanted to move swiftly. Their body pivoted at the hips, and their long tail counterbalanced their nearly erect trunk. This stance probably freed their forelimbs for attacking prey.

At the beginning of the Mesozoic era, about 240 million years ago, the dinosaurs descended from the thecodonts, two-legged reptiles, and many early dinosaurs developed a successful permanent bipedal stance. This increased their speed and agility and freed the forelimbs for foraging and other useful tasks that clumsy legs were unable to perform. It also meant that the back legs and hip had to support the entire weight of the animals, which probably kept them from growing larger than they did. Some of the bipedaled dinosaurs later reverted to a four-legged stance, probably as a result of increased weight, which eventually gave rise to the gigantic apatosaurus.

Dinosaur tracks (Figure 49) are the most spectacular of all fossil foot-prints, and they are found in relative abundance in terrestrial sediments of Mesozoic age in most parts of the world. Indeed, the climate during this time was mild enough to allow the migration of dinosaurs to just about every corner of the globe. Through time, the tracks of many dinosaurs show a lengthening of the stride, a narrowing of the trackway, and the pointing of the toes forward, all indications of increasingly efficient and fast locomotion. Some of the tracks were nearly mammal-like in their structure, possibly indicating an intermediate species between reptile and mammal. By the end of the Mesozoic, dinosaur footprints disappeared entirely from the face of the Earth, and there became a preponderance of mammal tracks.

Figure 49 A fossil dinosaur footprint in Dakota sandstone, Jefferson County, Colorado. The formation of a fossil footprint requires deep, distinct impressions, which are later filled with sediment and lithified into solid rock.

When the dinosaurs became extinct, the mammals were poised to take over the world. At first, the majority of mammals were small, nocturnal creatures with a limited range. Although they probably left numerous tracks, their light weight produced shallow footprints that did not fossilize well. As the mammals became larger, they left a better fossil record of their comings and goings.

In 1976, at Laetoli, Tanzania, well-preserved footprints of a large mammal were found embedded in a volcanic ash bed that was dated at 3.8 million years old. The footprints had rounded heals and arches, pronounced balls, and forward-pointing toes, all indications of an efficient form of locomotion. In addition, the tracks clearly showed that the animal preferred a bipedal walk. The most astonishing fact was that these fossil footprints were from one of our ancient ancestors who walked upright much earlier than was ever thought possible.

In the next two chapters, we will take a closer look at some of these marine and terrestrial fossils.

5

MARINE FOSSILS

The discovery, reliable dating, and piecing together of marine fossils have provided us with a fascinating window into the earliest forms of animal life on Earth. Among the most primitive creatures were microorganisms that built stromatolite structures (Figure 50). Ancestors of blue-green algae built these concentrically layered mounds, resembling cabbage heads, by cementing sediment grains together using a gluelike substance secreted from their bodies. As with modern stromatolites, the ancient stromatolite colonies grew in the intertidal zone, and their height, which was as much as 30 feet, was indicative of the height of the tides during their lifetime. This is because stromatolites grow between the low tide water mark and the high tide water mark. Since they reveal that the tides were so much higher than they are today, this suggests that the moon was much closer to the Earth and exerted a stronger gravitational pull.

By counting the layers in stromatolite fossils, researchers have estimated that there were approximately 435 days in a year (the time it takes the Earth to complete one revolution around the sun) during the late Proterozoic. This indicated that the Earth was spinning faster on its axis and that the days were only 20 hours long. The Earth's rotation rate gradually slowed as it gave up some of its angular momentum to the moon, sending it into a wider orbit. In addition, the ancient stromatolites provide information on the Earth's axis of rotation, which during the late Proterozoic tilted 26.5 degrees, compared with 23.5 degrees today. This supports the idea that the axial tilt angle has been decreasing with time.

PROTOZOANS

Paleontologists are generally divided into two classes: lumpers and splitters. The lumpers like to place all types of similar organisms into a single taxonomic category, whereas the splitters prefer many separate groupings. Some classification schemes place the protozoans in the kingdom of Protistae, which includes all single-celled plants and animals that possess a nucleus; in the obscured past, there were few distinctions among the earlier plants and animals, and they shared similar characteristics. Other classification schemes prefer to place the protozoans squarely in the animal kingdom, and indeed, protozoan literally means "beginning animal."

The ability to move about under their own

Figure 50   Stromatolite structure near the junction of Canyon Creek and Salt River, Gila County, Arizona. Photo 2 by A. F. Shride, courtesy USGS

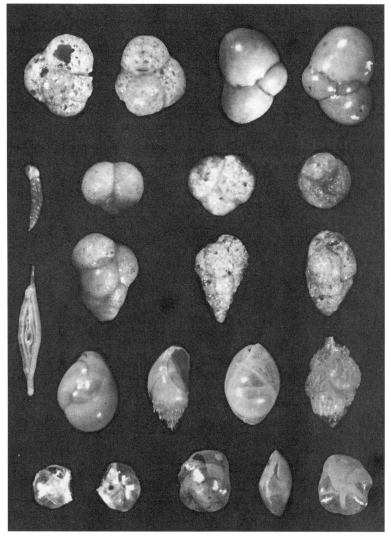

Figure 51   Foraminifera from the North Pacific Ocean. Photo 1 by R. B. Smith, courtesy USGS

power is what essentially separates animals from plants. Some unicellular animals moved about with a thrashing tail, called a flagellum, which resembled a filamentous bacteria that joined with the single-celled animal for mutual benefit. Other cells had tiny hairlike appendages, called cilia, which helped them travel by rhythmically beating the water. Amoeba moved by extending fingerlike protrusions outward from the main body and flowing into them.

The major fossil groups of protistids are algae, diatoms, dinoflagellates, radiolaria, and foraminifera. Because of their lack of a hard shell, the amoeba and paramecium did not fossilize well. Some varieties of protistids formed large colonies, but most lived independently. The organisms ranged from the Precambrian to the present, although many did not become well established until the Cambrian or later. The forams (Figure 51) are particularly useful to petroleum geologists, who use them for dating the stratigraphy of oil well cuttings.

Although individually, the protistids did not leave fossils that are of interest to most amateur collectors, they did perform a major function by building massive formations of limestone, which entombed other fossils. When the tiny organisms died, their shells fell to the ocean floor like a constant rain. The shifting of these sediments by storms and undersea currents buried dead marine organisms that were not eaten by scavengers. A calcite ooze was then formed, which eventually hardened into limestone, preserving trapped species permanently.

SPONGES

As time progressed, individual cells joined to form multicellular animals called metazoans, which evolved in the latter part of the Proterozoic, around 750 million years ago. The first metazoans were a loose organization of cells united for a common purpose such as locomotion, feeding, and protection. If cells became separated from the main body, they could exist on their own until they regrouped.

The most primitive metazoans were probably composed of a large aggregate of cells, each with its own flagellum. The cells were grouped into a small, hollow sphere, and their flagellum rhythmically beat the water to propel the tiny creature around. Some metazoans were literally turned inside out and attached themselves to the ocean floor. They had openings to the outside, and the flagella, now on the inside, produced a flow of water that carried food particles in and wastes out. These were probably the forerunners of the sponges.

The earlier sponges grew to enormous size, and some species were as much as 10 feet or more across (Figure 51a). The body consisted of three weak tissue layers,

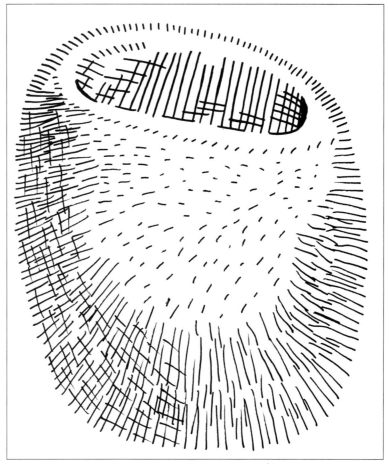

Figure 51a   The sponges were the first giants of the sea, growing 10 feet or more across.

whose cells were still capable of independent survival. If a sponge were cut into tiny pieces, each individual piece could grow into a new sponge. Certain groups had an internal skeleton of rigid, interlocking spicules composed of calcite or silica. Sponges ranged from the Precambrian to the present, but microfossils of sponge spicules did not become abundant until the Cambrian.

COELENTERATES

An evolutionary step above the sponges was the jellyfish. Two layers of cells separated by a gelatinous substance gave its saucerlike body a means of support. Unlike those of the sponges, the cells of the jellyfish were incapable of independent survival and were linked by a primitive nervous system that enabled them to contract in unison. These cells thus became the first simple muscles used for locomotion. Jellyfish ranged from the top of the Precambrian to the present, but because they lacked hard body parts they are rare as fossils and usually are only preserved as carbonized films or impressions.

More advanced than the jellyfish are the corals, which exist in a large variety of forms. Many are well represented in the fossil record, leaving fossils that looked similar to their modern counterparts (Figure 52). The corals began constructing reefs in the lower Paleozoic, forming entire chains of islands and altering the shoreline of the continents. The corals also built atolls on top of extinct marine volcanoes, and as the volcanoes subsided beneath the sea the rate of growth of the coral matched the rate of subsidence, which kept them at a constant depth.

The coral polyp is a soft-bodied creature that is essentially a contractible sac, crowned by a ring of tentacles (Figure 53). The tentacles surround a mouthlike opening and are tipped with poisonous stingers. The polyps live in individual skeletal cups composed of calcium carbonate. They extend their tentacles to feed at night and withdraw into their cups during the day or at low

Figure 52 Coral at Bikini Atoll, Marshall Islands. Photo 4 by K. O. Emery, courtesy USGS

tide to keep from drying out in the sun. The corals coexist in symbiosis with zooxanthellae algae, which live within the polyp's body. The algae consume the coral's waste products and produce organic materials that are absorbed by the polyp. Because the algae require sunlight for photosynthesis, corals must live in warm, shallow water.

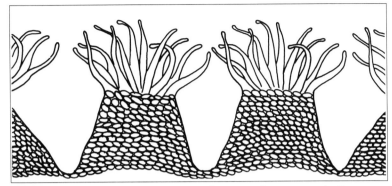

Figure 53   The coral polyps shown here require warm, shallow seas for photosynthesis of symbiotic algae.

The archaeocyathans resemble both corals and sponges. They formed the earliest reefs and became extinct in the Cambrian. The tabulate corals, which became extinct at the end of the Paleozoic, consisted of closely packed polygonal or rounded tubes, some of which had pores covering their walls. The rugose, or horn corals, so named because of their typical hornlike shape, were the major reef builders of the late Paleozoic and became extinct in the early Triassic. The hexacorals, which ranged from the Triassic to recent times, were the major reef builders of the Mesozoic and Cenozoic eras.

Today, many plant and animal communities thrive on the coral reef due to the coral's ability to build massive wave-resistant structures. In the geologic past, these structures were lithified into limestone, creating some of the greatest fossil deposits on Earth.

BRYOZOANS

The bryozoans are similar to corals, but comprise microscopic individuals living in small colonies up to several inches across, which give the ocean floor a mosslike appearance. Like corals, bryozoans live encased in a calcareous vaselike structure, retreating into the structure for protection. The polyp has a circle of ciliated tentacles, forming a sort of net around the mouth and used for filtering microscopic food floating by. Bryozoans have been very abundant, ranging from the Ordovician to the present, and their fossils are highly useful for making rock correlations.

Fossil bryozoans resemble their modern descendants, and some larger groups might have contributed to Paleozoic reef building. They are most abundant in limestone and less so in shales and sandstones. Fossils are common in Paleozoic formations, especially in the Midwest. Cenozoic

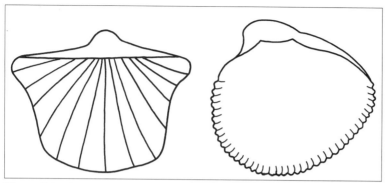

Figure 54 A comparison between the shells of brachs (left) and clams (right).

fossil shells might also contain a delicate outline of encrusting bryozoans. Because of their small size, bryozoans make ideal microfossils for dating oil well cuttings.

BRACHIOPODS

The most common fossils, found just about everywhere, are the brachiopods, or lamp shells. Primitive forms called inarticulates had two saucerlike shells, or valves, fitted face to face and opened and closed using simple muscles. The shells were not hinged and are often found as separate halves. More advanced species called articulates are similar to those living today. They had ribbed shells of unequal size and shape, which were symmetrical down the center line with interlocking teeth that opened and closed along a hinge line.

Brachiopods ranged from the Cambrian to the present, but were most abundant in the Paleozoic and to a lesser extent in the Mesozoic. They are important as guide fossils and are used to date many Paleozoic rocks. The occurrence of abundant brachiopods indicates seawater of moderate to shallow depth. The brachiopods were sometimes attached to the ocean floor by a footlike appendage and fed by filtering food particles through their open shells. Brachiopod shells are often confused with clam shells (Figure 54), which are also bivalved but belong to the more advanced mollusks. Clam shells are typically left and right in relation to the body, and are mirror images of each other with each valve being asymmetrical down the center line.

MOLLUSKS

The mollusks are probably the most common and diverse group of fossils. The phylum is so diverse it is often difficult to find common features among its members. The three major groups include snails, clams, and cephalopods. The mollusk shell is an ever-growing one-piece coiled structure for most species and a two-part shell for clams and oysters. Mollusks have a large muscular foot for creeping and burrowing, or it has been modified into tentacles for seizing prey. Snails and slugs are the largest fossil group, and ranged throughout the Phanerozoic.

The clams are generally burrowers, although many are attached to the ocean floor. The shell consists of two valves that hang down along either side of the body, and, except for scallops and oysters, they are mirror images of each other. The cephalopods, which include squid, cuttlefish, octopus, and nautilus, travel by jet propulsion. The animals suck water into a cylindrical cavity through openings on each side of the head and expel it under pressure through a funnel-like appendage.

The extinct nautiloids grew to lengths of 30 feet

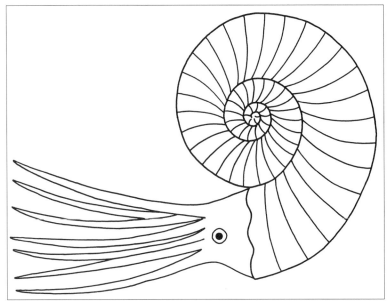

Figure 55   The ammonoids were among the most spectacular creatures of the Paleozoic and Mesozoic seas, some growing up to 7 feet long.

and more, and with their straight, streamlined shells they were among the swiftest and most spectacular creatures of the deep. The belemnoids were abundant during the Jurassic and Cretaceous and became extinct in the Paleogene. The chambered part of the belemnoid shell was smaller than the ammonoid and the outer walls were thickened into a fat cigar shape. The extinct ammonoids are the most significant cephalopods, with a large variety of coiled shell forms (Figures 55 and 56) that made them ideal for dating Paleozoic and Mesozoic rocks. Some ammonoids grew to tremendous size, with shells up to 7 feet across.

ANNELIDS

The annelids include marine worms, earthworms, and leaches. Early forms of marine flatworms grew very large, nearly 3 feet long, but were less than 1/10 inch thick. The animals were extremely flat in order to absorb directly into their bodies nutrients and oxygen from the ocean waters, present in only a small percentage of what they are today.

The primitive segmented worms, which were characterized by a repetition of similar parts in a series, developed muscles and other rudimentary organs, including sense organs and a central nervous system. The annelids ranged from the upper Precambrian to the present. Their fossils are rare and consist mostly of tiny teeth and jaws along with a preponderance of fossilized tracks, trails, and burrows.

ARTHROPODS

The arthropods form the largest group of animals, living or extinct, and they make the most fascinating fossils. The arthropods conquered land, sea, and air and are found in every environment on Earth. The body of an arthropod is segmented, which suggests a relationship to the annelid worms. Paired, jointed limbs are generally present on most segments and are modified for sensing, feeding, walking, and reproduction. One giant arthropod found in the middle Cambrian Burgess Shale Formation of western Canada was as much as 3 feet long. The crustaceans are primarily aquatic and include shrimp, lobsters, barnacles, and crabs (Figure 57). Of particular importance to geologists are the ostracods, or mussel shrimp, which are used for correlating rocks from the Ordovician onward.

Figure 56 Cretaceous ammonite fossils on display at the Museum of Geology, South Dakota School of Mines at Rapid City.

The arachnids comprise mostly air-breathing species and include spiders, scorpions, daddy longlegs, ticks, and mites. One giant Paleozoic sea scorpion had massive claws and grew over 6 feet long. The extinct eurypterids (Figure 58), which ranged from the Ordovician to the Permian, were also giants that grew up to 6 feet long. The insects are by far the largest living group of arthropods. They have three pairs of legs and, typically, two pairs of wings on the thorax, or midsection. To fly, insects have to be lightweight; therefore, their delicate bodies do not fossilize well, except when they were trapped in tree

Figure 57   Mesozoic fossils, with fossilized crabs in the foreground at the Museum of Geology, South Dakota School of Mines at Rapid City.

sap, which altered into amber. In most cases, the insect body is covered by an exoskeleton made of chitin, which is similar to cellulose and covers the outside of the body and the appendages. In some groups, the exoskeleton is composed of calcite or calcium phosphate, which greatly improved the animal's chances of fossilization.

The Cambrian is best known for the trilobites (Figure 59), which appeared at the base of the period and became the dominant species of the early Paleozoic. Because trilobites were so widespread

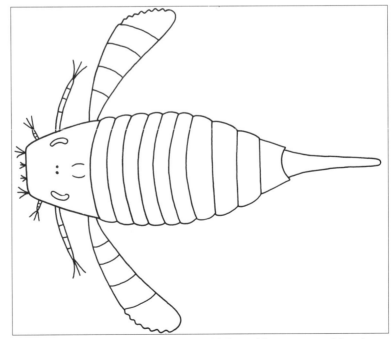

Figure 58   The extinct eurypterid, which could grow up to 6 feet long.

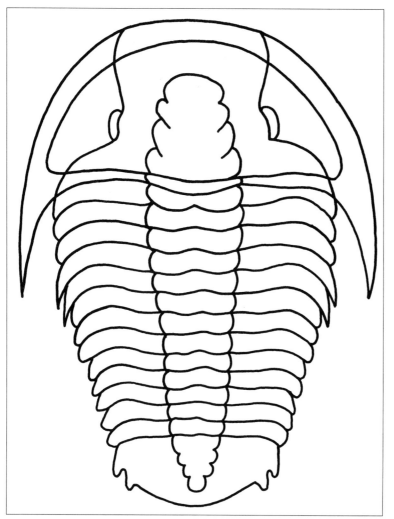

Figure 59 Trilobites, extinct ancestors of the horseshoe crab, make prized fossils.

and lived throughout the Paleozoic, their fossils are important markers for dating rocks of that era. Trilobites are thought to be primitive ancestors of the horseshoe crab, the only remaining direct descendent alive today. The giant paradoxides extended nearly 2 feet in length, but most trilobites were 0.5 to 4 inches long. The trilobite is divided into three lobes (hence its name), which include the head, body, and abdomen. Because trilobites shed their exoskeleton as they grow, most finds consist of only portions, and complete skeletons are harder to find.

Because arthropods must shed their outer skeletons in order to grow, it is possible that a single individual could leave several fossils behind. Arthropods ranged from early Cambrian (possibly late Precambrian) to the present.

ECHINODERMS

The echinoderm, meaning "spiny skin," is unique among the more complex animals in that it has fivefold radial symmetry. Echinoderms are also the only animals to have a system of internal canals, called a water vascular system, that operates a series of tube feet used for locomotion, feeding, and respiration. The great success of the echinoderms in thriving in their environment is illustrated by the fact that there are more classes of this animal both living and extinct than of any other phylum. The five major classes of living echinoderms include starfish, brittle stars, sea urchins, sea cucumbers, and sea lillies. The fossil record of the echinoderms goes back to the Cambrian and possibly late Precambrian.

The crinoids (Figures 60 and 61), known as sea lillies, became the dominant echinoderms of the middle and upper Paleozoic, and some species still exist. They had long stalks, some over 10 feet in length composed of up to 100 or more calcite disks, and were anchored to the ocean floor by a rootlike appendage. Perched on top of the stalk was a cup called a calyx that housed the digestive and reproductive systems. Food particles were strained from passing water currents by five feathery arms that extended from the cup, giving the animal a flowerlike appearance. The extinct Paleozoic crinoids and their blastoid relatives, whose calyx resembled a rosebud, made excellent fossils, especially the stalks, which on weathered limestone outcrops look like large strings of beads.

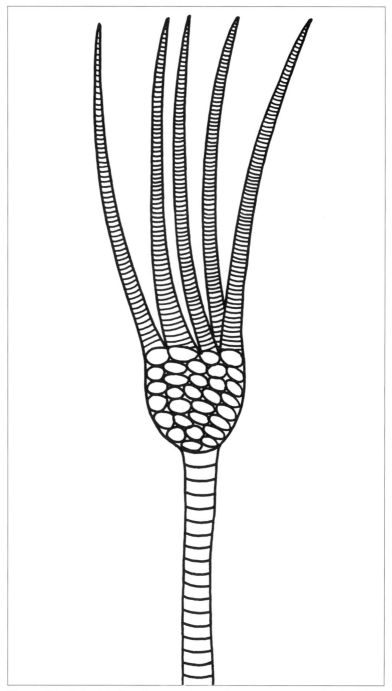

Figure 60 **Crinoids like the one shown here grew upwards of 10 feet tall.**

The starfish are common today and left fossils in Ordovician rocks of central and eastern United States. They have skeletons composed of tiny plates that are not rigidly joined together. As a result, the skeleton usually disintegrated when the animal died, making whole starfish fossils rare. The sea cucumbers, so named because of their shape, have large tube feet modified into tentacles. They have a skeleton composed of isolated plates, which are occasionally common as fossils.

One of the most significant fossil groups are the echinoids, which include sea urchins, heart urchins, and sand dollars. The sea urchins lived mostly among rocks encrusted with algae, upon which they fed. Unfortunately, by its very exposure such an environment was not conducive to fossilization. The familiar sand dollars, which occasionally wash up on beaches, likewise are rare in the fossil record.

Figure 61 • **Cogwheel-shaped crinoid columnals in a limestone bed of the Drowning Creek formation, Fleming County, Kentucky.** Photo 2 by R. C. McDowell, courtesy USGS

From fossil specimens, we have learned that there were also a number of strange animals that have defied efforts to classify them into existing phyla. One of these animals, appropriately named hallucigenia (Figure 62), propelled itself across the ocean floor on seven pairs of pointed stilts. Seven tentacles arose from the upper body, and each appeared to contain its own mouth. Another odd animal had five eyes arranged across its head, a vertical tail fin to help steer it across the seafloor, and a grasping

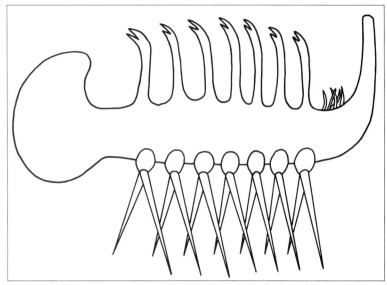

Figure 62 The aptly named hallucigenia is one of the strangest animals preserved in the fossil record. It walked on seven pairs of stilts and had seven tentacles, each with its own mouth.

organ projected forward for catching prey. One worm had enormous eyes and prominent fins. The conodonts, which resemble jawlike objects, are among the most puzzling of all fossils and are thought to be parts of an unusual soft-bodied animal.

Graptolites, colonies of cupped organisms that resembled stems and leaves, look much like plants but were actually animals. They were fixed to the ocean floor like small shrubs, floated freely near the surface, or were attached to seaweed. Large numbers of these organisms were buried in the bottom mud and fossilized into carbon, producing organic-rich black shales. This strata is so common the world over that graptolites are the most important group of fossils for long-distance time correlation of the lower Paleozoic.

VERTEBRATES

The marine vertebrates are represented by the fishes, which are a highly successful and diverse group. The first protofish were jawless, generally small (about the size of a minnow), and were heavily armored with bony plates. Although well protected from their invertebrate enemies, the added weight kept these fish mostly on the bottom, where they sifted mud for food particles and expelled the waste through slits on both sides of the throat, which later became gills. Gradually, the protofish acquired jaws with teeth, the bony plates gave way to scales, lateral fins developed on both sides of the lower body, and air bladders were used for buoyancy.

The Devonian period has been popularly called the "age of the fishes," and the fossil record reveals so many and varied kinds of fish that paleontologists have a difficult time classifying them all. Fish make up over half the species of vertebrates, both living and extinct. They include the jawless fish—lampreys and hagfish; the cartilaginous fish—sharks, skates, rays, and ratfish—and the bony fish—salmon, swordfish, pickerel, and bass. All major classes of fish alive today had ancestors in the Devonian, but not all Devonian fishes made it to the present. The extinct placoderms were fearsome giants, reaching 30 feet and more in length. The coelacanths (Figure 63), which are called "living fossils," are an exception to this rule. Thought to be extinct for 70 million years, a 6-foot coelacanth was caught in deep water off the South African coast in 1938. The fish looked ancient, a sort of castaway from the past, with a fleshy tail, a large set of forward fins behind the gills, powerful square, toothy jaws, and heavily armored scales. The remarkable thing about the catch was that this fish had not changed significantly from fossils of its 460-million-year-old ancestors.

The sharks were highly successful from the Devonian to the present. Instead of skeletons made of bone, which other fish have, sharks utilize cartilage, a more elastic and lighter material. Cartilage does not fossilize well, however, and as a result, about the only common remains of ancient sharks are their teeth, which can be found in relative abundance in rocks of Devonian age onward. Closely related to the sharks are the rays, which are substantially flattened with pectoral fins enlarged into wings that are up to 20 feet across and a tail reduced to a thin, whiplike appendage.

Finally, establishing connecting links between the fishes and terrestrial vertebrates were the Devonian crossopterygians and lungfish, another living fossil still in existence today. The crossopterygians were lobe-finned, meaning that the bones in their fins were attached to the skeleton and arranged into primitive elements of a walking limb. They could breath by taking air into primitive nostrils and lungs as well as by using gills, thereby placing them in the direct line of evolution from fish to land-living vertebrates.

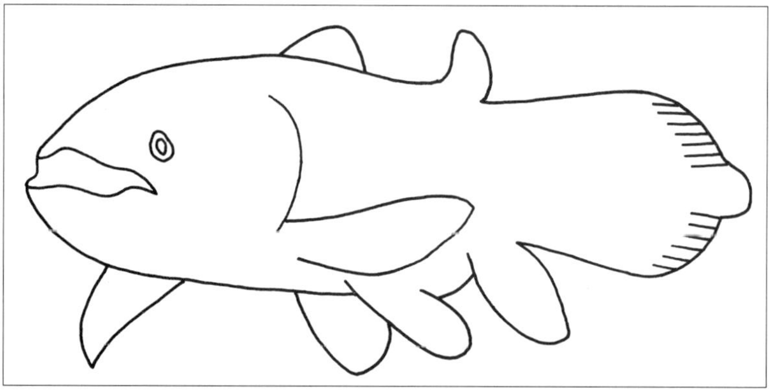

Figure 63 Modern coelacanths have not changed significantly from their 460-million-year-old ancestors.

6

TERRESTRIAL FOSSILS

Like animals, plants do not appear in the fossil record as complex organisms until the Cambrian, after which they began to evolve rapidly. The early seaweeds were soft and nonresistant and therefore did not fossilize well. Nevertheless, the Cambrian has been called the "age of the seaweed," even though this contention is not strongly supported by fossil evidence. A variety of fossil spores used for reproduction have been found in late Precambrian and Cambrian sediments, which suggests that complex sea plants were in existence, but there are no other significant remains. Even as late as the Ordovician, plant fossils appeared to be composed almost entirely of algae, which probably formed algal mats similar to those found on seashores today. Once life crept ashore, however, it did not take long before the entire Earth's surface was covered by lush forests.

It seems strange that life had been in existence for over three-quarters of the Earth's history before it conquered the land some 450 million years ago. Part of the reason might be that the level of oxygen in the Earth's atmosphere during this time was not high enough to form an effective ozone screen. The ozone layer, which lies between 25 and 30 miles altitude, filters out harmful ultraviolet rays from the sun. The strong ultraviolet radiation probably kept life in the protective waters of the oceans until such a time when the concentration of ozone became high enough to make it safe to venture out on dry land. This has significant implications for us today, for if we destroy the ozone layer by pumping pollution into the atmosphere, the land might once again be barren of life.

LAND PLANTS

Although terrestrial fossils are not nearly as abundant as marine fossils, primarily because the land is subjected to erosion, some environments like swamps and marshes provided an abundance of plant fossils. With the exclusion of simple algae and bacteria, plants are generally divided into two major subkingdom categories: Bryophyta, which includes mosses and liverworts, and Tracheophyta, which includes the higher plants that possess roots, stems, leaves, and flowers (Figure 64).

The simplest land plants, both living and extinct and among the first to live on shore, were the psilophytes, or whisk ferns. They had no roots or leaves, only stems. They lived half in and half out of the water and reproduced by using spores attached to the ends of simple limbs. When the spores matured, they were cast into the wind and carried to a suitable site, where they could grow into new adult plants.

The lycopods, which include the club mosses and scale trees, were the first to develop true roots and leaves. The leaves were generally small, and the branches were arranged in a spiral. The spores were attached to modified leaves that became primitive cones. The scale trees (Figure 65), so named because scars on their trunks resembled large fish scales, grew up to 100 feet tall and became one of the dominant trees of the Pennsylvanian period coal swamps.

As leaves became larger, branches had to be strengthened so they

Figure 64   Fossilized plants of the upper Pottsville series, Washington County, Arkansas. Photo 1559 by E. B. Hardin, courtesy USGS

would not break as the tree continued to grow. In order to maximize photosynthesis, the creation of carbohydrates by the reaction of sunlight, water, and carbon dioxide, leaves were exposed to as much sunlight as possible, placing further mechanical stress on the plant during wind storms. Therefore, those plants that developed an efficient branching pattern that gathered the most light were the most successful. The best branching pattern comprised tiers of branches similar to present-day pines. This pattern emerged during the first 50 million years of land plant life and remains highly successful today.

The second most diverse group of living plants are the true ferns. They ranged from the Devonian to the present and were particularly widespread in the Mesozoic, when they prospered in the mild climates, whereas today they are restricted to the tropics. Some ancient ferns attained heights of present-day trees. The

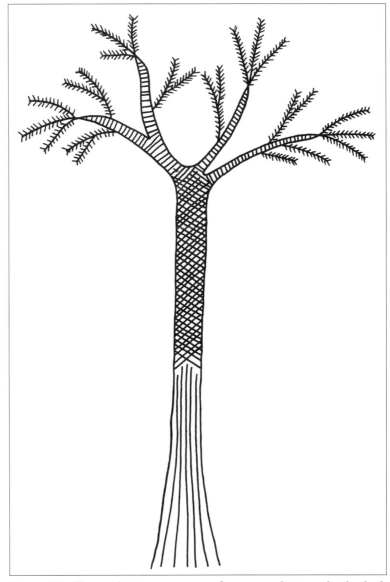

Figure 65 The scale tree was one of many early trees in the lush Carboniferous forest.

Permian seed fern glossopteris was especially significant for providing further evidence for continental drift. Its fossil leaves (Figure 66) were abundant on the southern continent of Gondwana but were suspiciously missing on the northern continent of Laurasia, indicating that the two megacontinents were once divided by the great Tethys Sea.

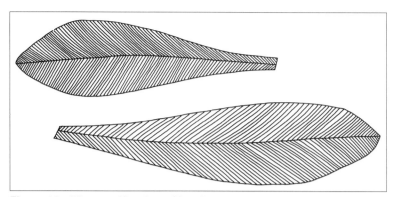

Figure 66   The stratification of fossil glossopteris leaves helped prove the theory of continental drift.

The cycads, which resembled palm trees, were highly successful during the Mesozoic and ranged across all major continents. They probably contributed significantly to the diets of the plant-eating dinosaurs. The ginkgo, of which the maidenhair tree in eastern China is the only living relative, might be the oldest genus of seed plants. Also dominating the Mesozoic forests were the conifers, some of which were nearly 400 feet high. Petrified trunks of conifers (Figure 67) were found to be as much as 5 feet wide and 100 feet long.

By far the largest group of plants in the world today are the angiosperms, or flowering plants. They were distributed worldwide by the end of the Cretaceous, and today they include about 250,000 species of trees, shrubs, grasses, and herbs. Flowering plants evolved alongside pollinating insects and offered them brightly colored and scented flowers along with sweet nectar. Many angiosperms also depended on animals to disperse their seeds, which were encased in fruit with an attractive taste. The seeds passed through the animal's digestive tract and were dropped some distance away.

It has been suggested that the rise of the angiosperms might have contributed to the demise of the dinosaurs at the end of the Cretaceous. The plants absorbed large amounts of atmospheric carbon dioxide, which could have resulted in a substantial drop in global temperatures. The opposite condition might be happening today as great rain forests are being cut down, diminishing their ability to remove excess carbon dioxide from the atmosphere, thereby raising global temperatures.

AMPHIBIANS

The first animals to crawl out of the sea were probably crustaceans, segmented creatures, ancestors of today's millipedes, that walked on perhaps 100 pairs of legs. At first, they remained near the shore and later moved farther inland along with the early mosses and lichens. Having the land to themselves with no competition or predation, these creatures found plenty to feed upon, and some grew to giants, 6 feet long. However, when relatives of the giant sea scorpion, eurypterid, took to the land, the ancestral millipedes, which were too slow, became easy prey.

With the advent of the forests, leaves and other edible parts were no longer near the ground within easy reach, posing serious problems for the ancestors of the insects. By developing winglike appendages, which might have been originally intended as cooling devices, insects were able to launch themselves into the forest canopy. The adaptation was particularly useful for escaping hungry amphibians, which were beginning to appear about this time.

The ancestors of the amphibians were the crossopterygians, which were encouraged to make short forays on shore to feed on abundant crustaceans and insects during the middle Devonian, about 300 million years ago. They began to strengthen their lobe fins into walking limbs by digging in the

Figure 67 **The three most prominent petrified tree stumps on North Scarp of Specimen Ridge in Yellowstone National Park, Wyoming.** Courtesy National Park Service

Figure 68   The rough evolution from crossopterygian (top) to the amphibians.

sand for food and shelter. This allowed them to venture farther inland, although not too far from accessible swamps or streams. By the early Mississippian, about 335 million years ago, these fish gave rise to the earliest amphibians (Figure 68). The amphibians still depended on a nearby source of water to moisten their skins and for reproduction since, like fish, they laid their eggs in water.

The early amphibians were slow and ungainly creatures, and their weak legs could hardly keep their squat bodies off the ground for any length of time. Thus, in order to become successful hunters without the need for speed or agility, the amphibians developed quite a remarkable tongue that could lash out at insects and flick them into their mouths. The adaptation worked so well that the amphibians quickly populated the Earth. But the necessity of having to live a semiaquatic life-style led to the eventual downfall of the amphibians when the great swamps began to dry up toward the end of the Paleozoic.

The amphibians continued to decline in the Mesozoic, with all large, flat-headed species becoming extinct early in the Triassic. The group thereafter was represented by the more familiar toads, frogs, and salamanders. The fossil remains of these amphibians are largely fragmentary, because vertebrate skeletons are constructed with numerous bones that are easily scattered by surface erosion.

REPTILES

The vacant spaces left behind by the amphibians were filled by their cousins, the reptiles, which were better suited for a life totally out of water. One of the reasons for the reptile's great success was its more efficient means of locomotion. The improvement over the amphibian foot included changes in the form of the toes, the addition of a short, thumblike fifth toe, and the appearance of claws. In addition, the reptile's toes pointed forward to allow the animal to run, whereas the amphibian's toes were splayed outward, making it slow and ungainly.

Reptiles have scales that retain the animal's bodily fluids, whereas amphibians have a permeable skin, which helps them breath. The skin of the amphibian also had to be moistened, and the animal would dry up if away from water for long periods. Reptiles lay their eggs, which have hard watertight shells, on dry land, whereas the amphibian's eggs do not have a protective membrane and, therefore, like fish eggs, had to be laid in water or moist places. Because the embryos took longer to develop, reptile eggs had to be protected from predators. This gave the young a better chance of survival, which contributed significantly to the reptile's great success in populating the land.

Like fish and amphibians, reptiles are cold-blooded, which does not mean their blood is always cold. Instead, the temperature of their bodies depends on the temperature of the environment, because reptiles have no means of regulating their body temperatures. Therefore, they are rather sluggish on cold mornings and must wait until the sun warms their bodies before they are able to reach their peak performance. The unusually warm climate of the Mesozoic must have contributed substantially to the success of the reptiles. In addition, reptiles only required a fraction of the amount of food that mammals need to survive, because mammals use most of their calories to maintain their high body temperatures.

The reptiles became the leading form of animal life on Earth and occupied land, sea, and air. The sea-cowlike placodonts, the sea-serpentlike plesiosaurs, and the dolphinlike ichthyosaurs (Figure 69) were reptiles that returned to the sea to compete with fish and achieved great success. Lizards and turtles also went to sea, and many modern giant turtles are descendants of those marine reptiles.

Perhaps the most spectacular reptiles that ever existed were the flying pterosaurs (Figure 70). They had wingspans of up to 40 feet, about the size of a small aircraft, and dominated the skies for 120 million years. Their wings were similar in construction to bat's wings with a finger on

Figure 69   The ichthyosaur was an air-breathing reptile that returned to the sea.

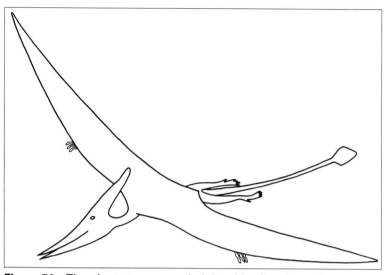

Figure 70   The giant pterosaur ruled the skies for 120 million years.

each forelimb greatly elongated and covered with a membrane that was attached along the side of the body. This appendage probably originated as a cooling mechanism, and the reptile regulated its body temperature by fanning its forelimbs. When the animal wanted to fly, it simply caught a breeze and with a single flap of its enormous wings and a kick from its powerful hind legs, it was airborne. It probably spent most of its time aloft riding updrafts like modern sailplanes.

By the close of the Triassic, a remarkable reptilian group appeared in the fossil record. These were the alligators and crocodiles. Members of this group adapted to life on dry land, a semiaquatic life, or a fully aquatic life. One marine species was about 15 feet in length and had a streamlined head, a sharklike tail, and legs molded into swimming paddles. Fossil crocodiles were among the first vertebrates unearthed by early 19th-century paleontologists and were used to support Charles Darwin's theory of evolution. Fossil alligators and crocodiles are found in the higher latitudes as far north as Labrador, indicating an unusually warm climate during the Cretaceous.

DINOSAURS

Dinosaurs descended from the thecodonts, the same common ancestors of crocodiles and birds, making them distant living relatives of the dinosaurs. The dinosaurs are classified into two major groups: the sauropods, which were mostly herbivores, and the carnosars, which were mostly carnivores. Not all dinosaurs were giants, and many were no larger than most modern mammals. The smallest known dinosaur footprints are only about the size of a penny. The smaller dinosaurs had hollow bones similar to those of birds. Some had long, slender hind legs, long delicate forelimbs, and a long neck, and if it were not for a long tail their skeletons would have resembled those of ostriches.

Many of the smaller dinosaurs established a permanent two-legged stance, which increased their speed and agility and freed their forelimbs for more successful foraging. The large, two-legged carnivores were swift runners and highly aggressive. *Tyrannosaurus rex* (Figure 71), the greatest land carnivore that ever lived, stood on powerful hind legs with its forelimbs shortened to almost useless appendages.

There is a great debate raging today over whether dinosaurs were cold-blooded like reptiles or warm-blooded like mammals and birds. One argument in favor of warm-bloodedness contends that the skeletons of the smaller, lighter dinosaurs bear many resemblances to those of birds. Evidence for rapid juvenile growth, which is common among mammals, is found in the bones of some dinosaur species, possibly providing another sign of warm-bloodedness.

It is thought that some dinosaurs were swift and agile, requiring a high rate of metabolism that only a warm-blooded body could provide. The complex social behavior of the dinosaurs also might have been an evolutionary advancement that resulted from being warm-blooded. There is even the suggestion that the females of some species gave live birth. The major problem with the theory of warm-bloodedness is that at the end of the Cretaceous, when the climate supposedly grew colder, the warm-blooded mammals survived while the dinosaurs did not.

Some dinosaur species grew to such giants for probably the same reasons that the elephant and rhinoceros are so large. The majority of the large dinosaurs were herbivores, or plant eaters, and therefore had to consume huge quantities of coarse cellulose, which took a long time to digest. This required a large stomach for the fermentation process and, consequently, a large body to carry it around. Some species swallowed gizzard stones (like modern birds do) in order to grind the fibrous fronds into pulp. The rounded, polished stones were left in a heap where the dinosaur died, and deposits of these stones can be found on top of exposed Mesozoic sediments, especially in the West.

Figure 71 *Tyrannosaurus rex* **was the greatest land carnivore that ever lived.**

Because large reptiles possess the power of almost unlimited growth, they continue to grow throughout their lives. A large body helps cold-blooded animals maintain their body temperature for long periods. This makes the animal less susceptible to short-term temperature variations in the environment. The only thing that kept the dinosaurs from growing larger than they did was the force of gravity. When an animal doubles its size, the weight on its bones quadruples. The only exception were the dinosaurs that lived permanently in the sea, and as with present-day whales, some of which are larger than the largest dinosaur that ever lived, the buoyance of seawater kept the weight off their bones.

One of the reasons why the dinosaurs were so successful is that they might have nurtured and fiercely protected their young, thus allowing a greater number to mature into adulthood. The parents might have brought food to their young, regurgitating seeds and berries similar to the way modern birds do. Some giant herbivores might have traveled in large herds with the juveniles kept in the middle for protection. Fifteen-foot-tall duck-billed hadrasaurs (Figure 72) lived in the arctic regions of the Northern and Southern Hemispheres, and either they adapted to the cold and the dark or migrated long distances to warmer regions. Dinosaurs are also thought to have been fairly intelligent and were able to react to environmental pressures, which explains why they dominated the planet for as long as they did.

The success of the dinosaurs is exemplified by their extensive range, in which they occupied a wide variety of ecologic niches and dominated all other forms of land animals. Roughly 500 species have been identified, although this is probably only a fraction of the total. Dinosaurs are known to have ventured to all major continents, and their distribution is strong evidence for continental drift. After the continents broke apart in the Jurassic, the dinosaurs could no longer cross from one continent to another and certain species are no longer found in some areas. Continental drift also might have contributed to the demise of the dinosaurs by rearranging the ocean basins, which redirected ocean currents, thereby changing global atmospheric patterns and bringing on unstable climatic conditions.

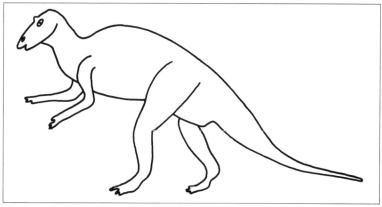

Figure 72 Fossil bones of hadrasaur found in Alaska suggest the dinosaur might have migrated south when the climate grew cold.

At the end of the Creta-
ceous, the dinosaurs
along with 70 percent of
all known species be-
came extinct. Because
the boundary between
the Cretaceous and the
Tertiary, called the K-T
boundary, is not a sharp
break but might repre-
sent up to a million years
or more, this dying out
was not necessarily sud-
den but could have taken
place over an extended
period. Many dinosaurs

Figure 73   Vast herds of triceratops roamed all parts of the world toward the end of the Cretaceous period.

along with other species were already in decline several million years prior
to the end of the Cretaceous. Triceratops (Figure 73), whose vast herds
covered the entire globe and might have contributed to the decline of other
dinosaur species, were among the last dinosaurs to go.

BIRDS

Birds first appeared in the Jurassic, around 150 million years ago. They
descended from the same thecodonts that gave rise to the crocodilians and
the dinosaurs, and for this reason they have been called "glorified reptiles."
They also retain the reptilian mode of reproduction by laying eggs. Birds
are warm-blooded in order to obtain the maximum sustainable amount of
energy needed for flight, which requires a high metabolic rate.

The earliest known fossil bird is *Archaeopteryx* (Figure 74), about the
size of a crow. It was once thought to be a hoax by prominent 19th-century
scientists, who mistakenly claimed that feather impressions were engraved
on the fossil. *Archaeopteryx* had teeth, claws, a long tail, and many skeletal
features of a small dinosaur. Its feathers were outgrowths of scales that were
probably used originally for insulation. Thus, *Archaeopteryx* appeared to
be a species in transition between reptiles and birds, but it could not fly,
at least not very far.

After mastering the skill of flight, birds quickly radiated into all environments. Their greater adaptability allowed them to successfully compete
with the pterosaurs, which might have been a major factor in that reptile's
extinction. Giant flightless birds appeared very early in the fossil record.
Their wide distribution is further evidence for the existence of the super-

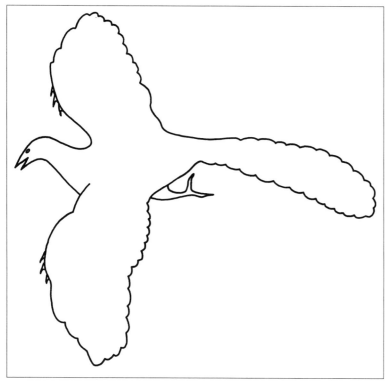

Figure 74 This *Archaeopteryx* **might be a link between reptiles and birds.**

continent of Pangaea since these birds had to travel on foot to get from one part of the world to another.

Having been driven into the air by the dinosaurs, birds, once the dinosaurs disappeared, found life a lot easier on the ground because they had to expend a great deal of energy in order to stay in the air. Some birds also successfully adapted to a life in the sea. Penguins are large flightless birds that have taken to life in the ocean and are well adapted to survive in the Antarctic. Certain diving ducks are especially equipped for "flying" underwater to catch fish.

MAMMALS

About 300 million years ago, the pelycosars became the first group of animals to depart from the basic reptilian stock. The 11-foot-long dimetrodon (Figure 75) had a large dorsal fin that was well supplied with blood and is believed to be the first attempt at regulating the body's temperature. As blood circulated through the sail, its temperature was lowered by cooler air in the atmosphere around it. When the climate became warmer, the pelycosars lost their sails and perhaps gained some degree of internal temperature control. The pelycosars thrived for about 50 million years and then gave way to the mammal-like reptiles called the therapsids.

The therapsids ranged in size from that of a mouse to a hippopotamus. Early members invaded Gondwana during the late Permian, when that continent was still recovering from an ice age, indicating that the animals might have been warm-blooded in order to survive the cold. As the more advanced therapsids moved into the colder regions, they developed fur in place of scales. They still retained the reptilian mode of laying eggs; however, they probably incubated their eggs and nurtured their young. The therapsids dominated animal life on Earth for more than 40 million years. Then for unknown reasons, they lost out to the dinosaurs and were relegated to a nocturnal life-style until the dinosaurs became extinct.

Of the dozen or more orders of mammals that existed after the extinction of the dinosaurs, only half were found in the preceding Cretaceous and only half are living today. Many of the archaic mammals, including some large, peculiar-looking animals, disappeared at the end of the Eocene, about 37 million years ago, when the planet took a plunge into a colder climate.

Afterward, truly modern mammals began to appear (Figure 76). The extremes in climate and geography during the Cenozoic era produced a large variety of living conditions and presented many challenging opportunities for the mammals.

Figure 75 This 300-million-year-old pelycosaur called dimetrodon used the huge back sails to regulate its body temperature.

Figure 76 Fossil mammal skeletons on display at the Museum of Geology, South Dakota School of Mines at Rapid City.

Continental drift isolated many groups of mammals, and they evolved along independent lines. Australia was inhabited by strange, egg-laying mammals called monotremes, which included the spiny anteater and the platypus, both of which rightfully should be classified as surviving mammal-like reptiles. Looking as though it were designed by a committee, the platypus has a duck's bill, webbed feet and a broad flattened tail, and lays eggs. The marsupials have pouches on their bellies for incubating their tiny young after birth. Marsupials originated in North America about 100 million years ago and migrated southward to Australia, using Antarctica as a land bridge (Figure 77). Camels also originated in North America in the early Miocene, and 2 million years ago, they migrated to other parts of the world by connecting land bridges, which were exposed during the Pleistocene Ice Ages.

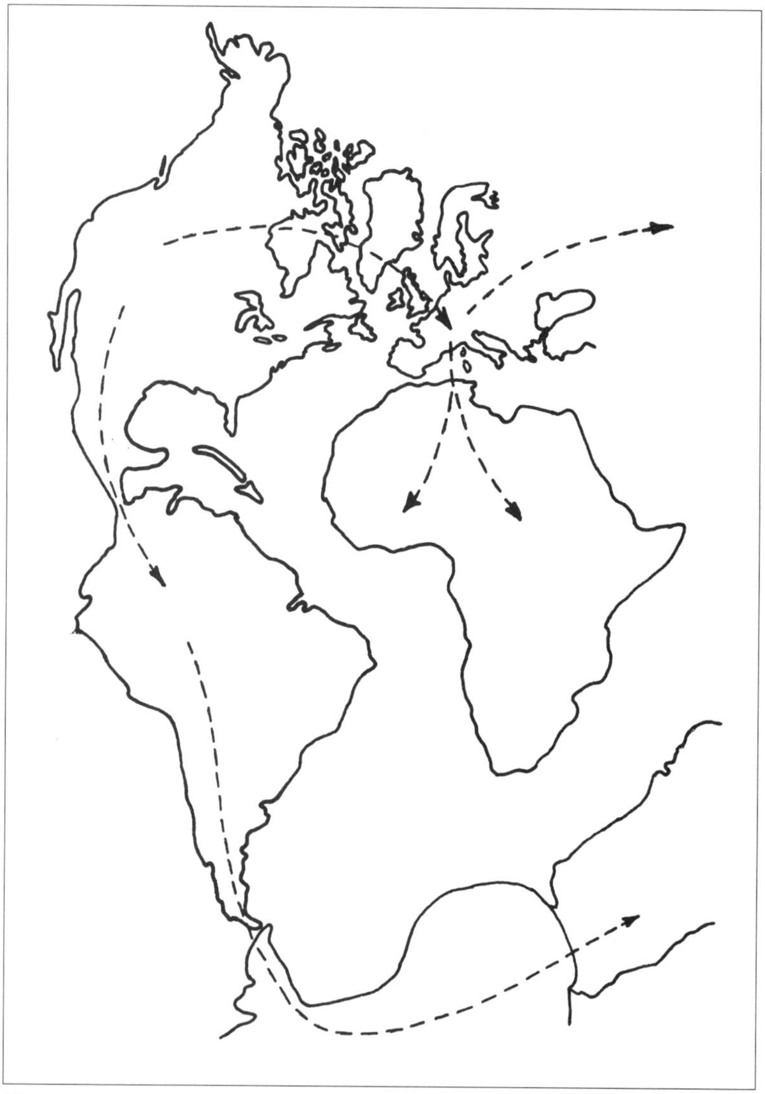

Horses originated in western North America during the Eocene, when they were only about the size of a small dog. As time went on, they became progressively larger, their faces and teeth grew longer as the animal switched from browsing from trees to grazing, and the toes fused into hoofs. In Africa, the giraffes grew long necks in order to browse on high branches, and the snouts of the elephants were elongated for similar reasons. These are cited as classic examples of evolution at work, adapting animals to their changing environment.

Figure 77 A map indicating the dispersion of marsupials to other parts of the world 80 million years ago.

Figure 78 Fossil mammoth bones on display at the Mammoth Site, Hot Springs, South Dakota.

During the last ice age, relatives of the elephant, the mammoth and mastodon, along with other mammals, like the giant sloth and saber-tooth cat, grew to enormous size and roamed the ice-free regions in many parts of the Northern Hemisphere. The giantism might have resulted from similar circumstances that led to the great size of some dinosaurs, including an abundant food supply and lack of predation. When the glaciers retreated, the change to a more seasonal climate broke up uniform environments, causing the forests to shrink and the grasslands to expand, which might have disrupted the food chains of several large mammals. It has also been suggested that by this time, man had become a successful hunter and decimated the slow, lumbering creatures, often wastefully, leaving their bones in great heaps (Figure 78).

7

CRYSTALS AND MINERALS

W e will now turn from a discussion of fossils to an examination of minerals. A *mineral* is a homogeneous substance, with a unique chemical composition and crystal structure. A *crystal* is an orderly growth of a mineral into a solid geometric form. Most minerals develop crystals, which greatly aid in their identification. The most abundant rock-forming minerals are quartz and feldspar, which make up the majority of the noncarbonate, or crystalline, rocks. When a magma body cools, a variety of minerals with varying crystal sizes separate out of the melt. This leaves behind highly volatile mineralized fluids that invade the rocks surrounding the magma chamber to form veins of ore, from which the mineral can be extracted.

Some of the larger, heavier crystals might sink to the bottom of the magma chamber to form very coarse-grained granitic rocks called pegmatites (from the Greek, meaning "fastened together"). Minerals are also formed by hydrothermal (hot water) activity, especially on the ocean floor. In many parts of the world, pieces of ocean crust that contain minerals have been shoved up on land by continental collisions. These are called ophiolites, and they provide important ore deposits (Figures 79 and 80).

Most minerals consist of two or more elements chemically united in a compound, such as silicon dioxide (SiO_2), which forms quartz. Feldspar,

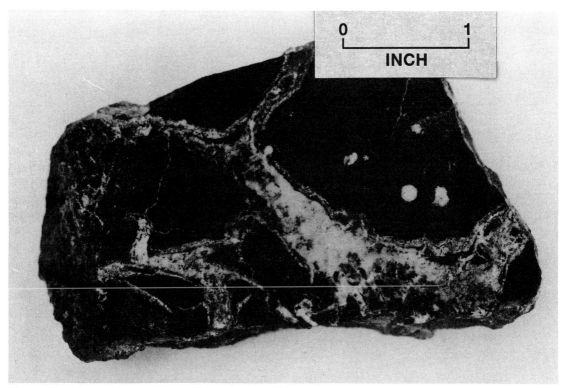

Figure 79   Metal-rich massive sulfide vein deposit in ophiolite. Photo 320 courtesy USGS

the most common mineral, constituting nearly half the Earth's crust, is composed of aluminum silicates, containing either sodium, calcium, or potassium. Single-element minerals can form metallic ores such as copper or nonmetallic substances such as sulfur, which is mostly associated with volcanic activity (Figure 81). Graphite, which is the most common form of carbon, has a layered structure with the chem-

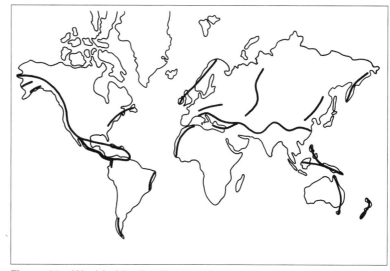

Figure 80   Worldwide distribution of ophiolites that originated on the ocean floor.

Figure 81   Sulfur deposits accumulating around a volcanic fumarole.
Photo courtesy USGS

ical bonding within each layer as strong as that of a diamond. Yet, the bonding between adjacent layers is so weak that graphite is soft enough to be used for pencil lead or as a lubricant.

CRYSTALS

Crystals are mostly empty space filled with an orderly arrangement of atoms or molecules, and the relative sizes of atoms determine how they fit together to form minerals. In crystals, atoms are arranged in a lattice of identical unit cells, which are the building blocks of the crystal and always contain the same distribution of atoms. Because oxygen exists in the greatest abundance and usually comprises the largest number of atoms present, it has the greatest influence on the growth of crystals. Crystals grow by continually adding layers of atoms over a template, or seed crystal, giving each mineral a unique set of crystal planes called faces. For example, large halite crystals (rock salt) can be grown in a container of supersaline sodium chloride solution by the submersion of a single tiny salt crystal.

A crystal's atoms are linked together by ionic bonding, whereby positively charged ions called cations are typically surrounded by negatively charged ions called anions. The cluster formed by a cation and its surrounding anions produces regular shapes, with the anions, usually oxygen ions, located on the corners of a polyhedron, such as a tetrahedron with four faces, a cube with six faces, or an octahedron with eight faces. Crystals seem hard because the electrical forces that bind widely scattered atomic nuclei together are extremely powerful. But even sturdy crystals can be compressed and reduced in volume by 50 percent or more when subjected to pressures equivalent to those near the center of the Earth. If the space in which a crystal is growing becomes crowded due to the rapid growth of other crystals around it, the crystal could cease growing entirely or continue growing abnormally. This is the major reason why large, perfect crystals are so rare.

The basic building blocks of a quartz crystal (Figure 82), the most common oxide of silicon, are tetrahedrons, composed of a silicon ion surrounded by four oxygen ions, situated on the four corners of a tetrahedron (Figure 83). Each of these shares four corners with four other tetrahedrons to form a continuous three-dimensional framework that is extremely rigid, thus making quartz among the hardest of the common minerals.

In a two-dimensional model of a crystal, an atom sits in the center of a hexagon, whose sides are formed by six of its closest neighbors. This hexagon is the unit cell of the crystal, and crystals can be broken down into a repeating pattern of hexagons. The hexagons in one part of the crystal have the exact same orientation, or alignment, as those in other parts of the crystal. In addition, if straight parallel lines are drawn connecting all atoms in a crystal, the lines will be evenly spaced across the crystal. Lines from one part of the crystal will match up precisely with lines in another part of the crystal. There are

Figure 82 Large quartz crystals. Photo 1436 by W. T. Schaller, courtesy USGS

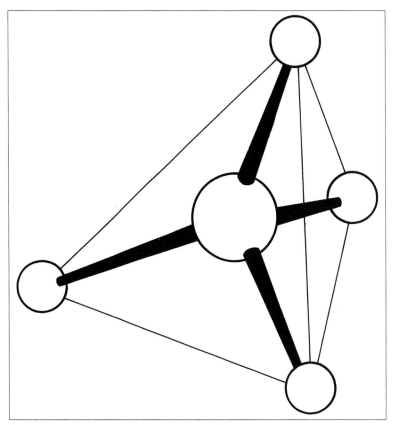

Figure 83   The basic building blocks of a quartz crystal are molecular tetrahedrons.

many families of these parallel lines, with each family facing a different direction. In a three-dimensional model of the crystal, these lines become planes called lattice planes.

Every crystal structure has certain symmetries. For example, a crystal has threefold rotational symmetry if the lattice of the crystal looks exactly the same after the crystal is rotated one third of a circle, or 120 degrees. An example of a shape that has threefold rotational symmetry is an equilateral triangle. Crystals might also have fourfold rotational symmetry like a square or sixfold rotational symmetry like a hexagon. But a natural crystal can never have fivefold rotational symmetry because shapes with fivefold rotational symmetry, such as pentagons, cannot be fitted together without leaving gaps (Figure 84). In nature, six-sided hexagons are used for many structures, from honeycombs to lava columns.

Crystals are generally classified according to the number, position, and length of their crystal axes (Figure 85). Isometric crystals like those of halite or galena have three perpendicular axes of equal length. Tetragonal crystals like those of zircon or cassiterite have three perpendicular axes with only two of equal length. Hexagonal crystals like those of quartz or calcite have three axes of equal length that meet at angles of 120 degrees and a fourth axis of a different length, perpendicular to the others. Orthorhombic crystals like those of topaz or olivine have three perpendicular axes all with different lengths. Monoclinic crystals like those of gypsum or orthoclase have three unequal axes, two that meet at oblique angles, and a third perpendicular to the other two. Triclinic crystals like those of plagioclase and microcline have three unequal axes that meet at oblique angles.

Some minerals can have the same chemical composition but different crystal structures due to different environments of deposition. Graphite, one of the softest minerals, and diamond, the hardest natural mineral, are both different forms of the element carbon but are subjected to different environmental conditions.

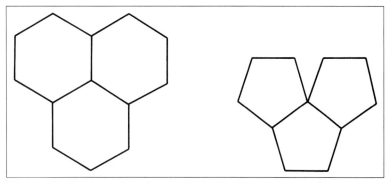

Figure 84 A comparison between the fit of hexagons and pentagons.

Twin crystals are two or more crystals of the same mineral that are united with interlocking adjacent parts so that the atomic structure is shared in common. They might grow parallel to each other, grow in opposite directions to each other, or grow in mirror images of each other (Figure 86). A

System	Cubic (isometric)	Tetragonal	Hexagonal	Orthorhombic	Monoclinic	Triclinic
Example						
Ideal shape						
Lengths of axes	All equal	Two horizontal equal – third different	Three equal horizontal axes – fourth axis different	Three axes – unequal	Three axes – unequal	Three axes – unequal
Axes of intersection	90°	90°	60° 90°	90°	Only two 90°	None 90°

Figure 85 The classification of crystals depends on their crystal axes, as shown here.

crystal of one mineral can change by metamorphism into another mineral of the same chemical composition by rearranging its atoms with no change in the crystal's external shape. A crystal of one mineral can also chemically change into another mineral by the addition or loss of elements with no change in the external shape of the crystal.

Crystal habit, or appearance, such as cubic, octahedral, or prismatic, is the form a crystal takes in response to temperature, pressure, and other factors in the geologic environment. Some minerals always develop a particular crystalline form, while others rarely develop well-formed geometric crystals. Crystals can be prismlike, needlelike, threadlike, bladelike, or sheetlike. They can also be branchlike, netlike, mosslike, or starlike. Crystals can form spherical or semispherical groups, long conic or columnar groups, or concentric groupings of platy, or layered, crystals. They can cover a surface with a layer of closely spaced tiny crystals, called drusy crystals. If crystals grow in restricted spaces, which occurs when magma cools rapidly, the crystal form might only be revealed under a microscope.

Figure 86   A twin gypsum crystal showing two halves that are mirror images of each other.

IDENTIFICATION OF MINERALS

Minerals are generally identified by crystal form, color, luster, hardness, density, cleavage, and fracture. Some minerals can also be recognized by transparency, tarnish, tenacity, iridescence, effervescence, fluorescence, magnetism, radioactivity, taste, or smell. In addition to these, geologists identify minerals by using elaborate laboratory equipment, including electron microscopes and x-ray diffraction machines, which provide information on crystal structure.

Because most minerals are comprised of crystals, the three-dimensional shape of a crystal offers one of the most important clues to identification. The outer arrangement of the plane surfaces reflects the inner structure of the crystal, which in turn is controlled by its chemical composition. If grown without obstruction, minerals develop a characteristic crystal form. But most minerals occur in irregular masses of small crystals due to restricted growth; therefore, perfect crystals are rare. Giant crystals are rarer still and reflect a deep-seated origin within the crust. One of the largest crystals was discovered at the Etta mine near Keystone, South Dakota. It was a prismatic spodumene crystal, of the pyroxene group, composed of lithium aluminum silicate and measured 42 feet long and weighed approximately 90 tons.

In addition to a crystal's form, its color, a result of the absorption and reflection of certain wave lengths of light, is another essential clue used for identification. Some minerals have a consistent color such as galena (gray), hematite (red), sulfur (yellow), azurite (blue), and malachite (green). Some minerals like quartz have a variety of hues, which are generally controlled by pigments or impurities. Weathering often changes the color of a mineral, and a fresh surface is required to determine its true color. Sometimes a mineral's true color does not show until it is ground to a powder or scraped across a piece of unglazed porcelain called a streak plate; therefore, this color is called the mineral's streak.

Besides its color, a mineral's luster, or the way it reflects light, is important for classifying minerals. The terms used for describing a mineral's luster are of common, everyday usage. A metallic luster is produced by most metals. A brilliant luster is like that of a diamond. Minerals with a glassy luster look like glass. A greasy luster looks oily. Minerals that have the look of resin have a resinous luster. A waxy luster has the appearance of wax. If a mineral has the iridescence of a pearl, it has a pearly luster. If a mineral is fibrous, it has a silky luster. A dull or earthy luster is like that of clay.

The hardness of a mineral is its resistance to scratching and is an important aid in identifying minerals. The hardness scale, also called the Mohs scale, named after the German mineralogist Friedrich Mohs who proposed it over a century ago, is an arrangement of 10 minerals according

TABLE 9 THE MOHS HARDNESS SCALE	
1. Talc	6. Orthoclase
2. Gypsum	7. Quartz
3. Calcite	8. Topaz
4. Fluorite	9. Corundum
5. Apatite	10. Diamond

to their hardness (Table 9). The softest mineral is talc, which was used for centuries as a lubricant and as talcum powder. The difference in hardness between corundum and diamond is quite large. However, the hardness of the others are fairly equally spaced along the scale. With this scale, the hardness of some common substances can be substituted for comparison: fingernail (2.5); copper penny (3.5); carpenter nail (4.5); knife blade (5.5); and steel file (6.5). When determining a mineral's hardness, one should be careful that a powdery residue is not mistaken for a scratch. Often cleaning the scratched area or reversing the test by scratching one with the other will determine which substance is harder.

The specific gravity or density of a substance is a measure of its relative weight compared with that of an equal volume of water and is expressed in grams per cubic centimeter. This measurement is made by first weighing the mineral in air and then in water (Figure 87). If the mineral weighed 2.0 units in air and 1.5 units in water, the difference of 0.5 unit is divided into the weight in air to yield a specific gravity of 4.0. Thus, if a mineral has a specific gravity of 4.0, it is four times as dense as water and therefore has a density of 4.0. Most nonmetallic minerals in the Earth's crust have densities between 2.5 and 3.0. Many common metallic minerals have densities over 5.0. The large difference between the densities of nonmetallic and metallic minerals becomes readily apparent when holding one of them in each hand.

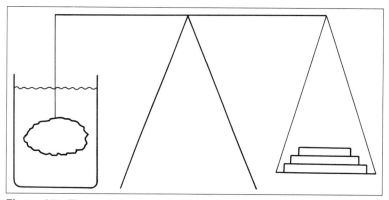

Figure 87   The weight of a substance immersed in water is less than it is in air, and the comparison of the two weights constitutes the specific gravity.

A mineral has cleavage if it splits along a smooth plain parallel to a crystal face. Usually, a hammer blow or prying with a knife blade will determine whether a mineral has cleavage. Perhaps one of the most recognizable minerals with excellent cleavage is mica, which splits easily into thin, flexible sheets. Gemologists who cut diamonds are well aware of cleavage patterns and study them very carefully before striking a large, valuable stone.

Minerals with little or no cleavage fracture along an irregular break when struck by a hammer. A common type of fracture is conchoidal, or

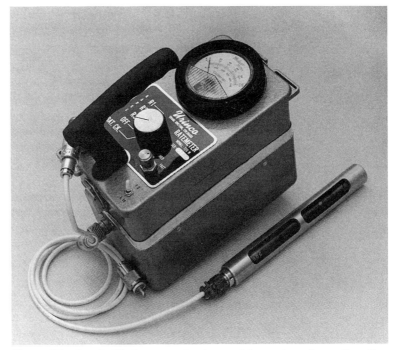

Figure 88   A scintillation counter is used to explore for radioactive minerals. Photo courtesy URINCO

shell-like, and shows concentric rings, typically like those on broken glass. Metals break leaving jagged edges and therefore have a hackly fracture. If a fracture is fairly smooth, it is an even fracture and if not smooth it is an uneven or rough fracture. A fibrous or splintery fracture resembles broken wood. If a mineral breaks like clay, it has an earthy fracture.

Other identifying features of minerals include taste, which can be tested with the tongue to identify halite; magnetism, which can be tested with a magnet to identify magnetite; effervescence, which can be tested with a weak hydrochloric acid solution to identify calcite; fluorescence, which is the absorption and reradiation of light that can be tested with a black light to identify zinc and tungsten minerals; and radioactivity, which is the emission of particles by the decay of radioactive elements that can be tested with a radiation counter (Figure 88) to identify uranium and thorium minerals.

THE ROCK-FORMING MINERALS

Of the nearly 2000 known minerals, only a few make up the majority of rocks found on the Earth's surface. The main rock-forming minerals are silicates, of which iron, magnesium, sodium, calcium or potassium have chemically combined with oxygen, silicon, and aluminum. Table 10 indicates the crystal abundance of rocks and minerals measured in percent volume of the entire crust.

TABLE 10   CRUSTAL ABUNDANCE OF ROCK TYPES AND MINERALS

Rock Type	Percent Volume	Minerals	Percent Volume
Sandstone	1.7	Quartz	12.0
Clays and shales	4.2	Potassium feldspar	12.0
Carbonates	2.0	Plagioclase	39.0
Granites	10.4	Micas	5.0
Grandiorite Quartz diorite	11.2	Amphiboles	5.0
Syenites	0.4	Pyroxenes	11.0
Basalts Gabbros Amphibolites Granulites	42.5	Olivine	3.0
		Sheet silicates	4.6
Ultramafics	0.2	Calcite	1.5
Gneisses	21.4	Dolomite	0.5
Schists	5.1	Magnetite	1.5
Marble	0.9	Other	4.9

Feldspars (Figure 89) are the most abundant minerals and exist in two varieties: one is an aluminum silicate of sodium or calcium called plagioclase, and the other is an aluminum silicate of potassium called orthoclase and microcline. Feldspars are an important component of granite and sandstone. They also decompose into kaolinite, or ordinary clay. Feldspars form monoclinic or triclinic crystals (see page 103) with a white or pink to dark gray color, and pearly to vitreous luster, a hardness of 6, a density of 2.6 to 2.8, and two cleavages at nearly right angles. In addition, plagioclase has fine striations on a cleavage surface.

Quartz, which is the most common mineral next to feldspar, forms six-sided, prismatic crystals with a clear to gray color as well as various hues, such as pink for rose quartz. Quartz crystals have a vitreous to greasy luster, a hardness of 7, a density of 2.6, and a conchoidal fracture. A type of quartz known as chalcedony is an important component of certain rocks, including flint, chert, and jasper.

Mica, which has perfect cleavage, comes in a clear variety called muscovite, a black variety called biotite, and a green variety called chlorite. Micas form orthohombic or hexagonal, scalelike crystals with a vitreous to pearly luster, a hardness of 2 to 3, and a density of 2.7 to 3.0. Micas are common in igneous, metamorphic, and sedimentary rocks.

Pyroxenes are a large group of complex minerals composed of silicates of calcium, magnesium, iron, and aluminum. Augite is the most common pyroxene and the main rock-forming mineral of the family. It forms stubby, eight-sided prismatic monoclinic or orthohombic crystals (see page 103) with a dark green to black color, a vitreous to dull luster, a hardness of 5 to 6, a density of 3.2 to 3.6, and two cleavages at right angles. Pyroxenes are common metamorphic rocks and are sometimes found in meteorites.

Amphiboles are another large group of complex minerals composed

Figure 89 Feldspar crystals in granite near Round Meadow of Tuolumne River, Yosemite National Park, Tuolumne County, California. The larest crystal is 5 inches in diameter. Photo 2060 by G. K. Gilbert, courtesy USGS

Figure 90   Hot carbonated spring water undercuts bedded travertine deposits at Yellowstone National Park, Wyoming. Photo 18 by K. E. Barger, courtesy USGS

of hydrated (combined with water) silicates of calcium, magnesium, iron, and aluminum. Hornblende is the most common amphibole and the main rock-forming mineral of the family. It forms long, slender, six-sided prismatic orthohombic or monoclinic crystals with a dark green to black color, a vitreous luster, a hardness of 5 to 6, a density of 2.9 to 3.2, and two cleavages at oblique angles. Amphiboles are common in basic igneous and metamorphic rocks. One variety used for insulation that has been in the news lately is asbestos.

Olivine is an iron-magnesium silicate and the simplest of the dark minerals. It has small, sugary grains, and crystals are relatively rare. Olivine has a distinctive olive green color (hence its name), a vitreous luster, a hardness of 6.5 to 7, a density of 3.2 to 3.5, and a conchoidal fracture. Olivine is an important constituent of many basic igneous and metamorphic rocks.

Calcite is a calcium carbonate and the most common mineral in limestone. It has dogtooth or flat, six-sided crystals with a clear to white color, but impurities can produce colors of yellow, green, orange, or brown. Calcite crystals have a vitreous or dull luster, a hardness of 3, a density of 2.7, and excellent cleavage in three directions. Another form of calcite, called travertine, is common in hot carbonate springs (Figure 90) and in caves. Calcite also forms in igneous vein deposits called carbonatites. It effervesces strongly in dilute hydrochloric acid.

Gypsum is a hydrated calcium sulfate and forms by the evaporation of seawater. It has tabular or fibrous monoclinic crystals with a clear or white color, a vitreous to pearly luster, a hardness of 2, a density of 2.3, and perfect cleavage with flexible but nonelastic flakes. Single crystals are found in black shales. A compact, massive form is known as alabaster.

Some of the common ore-forming minerals include hematite, which is distinguishable by its bloodred color and is the most abundant ore of iron (a mass of rock from which the iron is extracted). Pyrite, called "fool's gold" due to its similar golden appearance, is known for its cubic, brassy crystals. Chalcopyrite, another "fool's gold," is the most abundant ore of copper and often an ore of gold or silver. Galena with its heavy, gray cubic crystals is the most important ore of lead. Sphalerite forms yellowish to brownish cubic crystals with six perfect cleavages and is the most important ore of zinc. Cassiterite forms tetragonal pyramidlike crystals and is practically the sole ore of tin.

Figure 91   Pennsylvanian and Permian coal deposits in the United States.

ORE DEPOSITS

We have barely scratched the surface in the search for minerals. Immense resources lie at great depths awaiting the technology to bring them up to the surface.

Gold is mined on every continent except Antarctica. In Africa, the best gold deposits are in rocks as old as 3.4 billion years. In North America, the best gold mines are in the Great Slave region of northwest Canada, where there are over 1000 deposits in greenstone belts that were invaded by hot magmatic solutions from the intrusion of granitic bodies, and the gold occurs in veins associated with quartz.

Iron is the fourth most abundant element in the Earth's crust. Iron of Precambrian age was leached from the continents and dissolved in seawater under a reducing environment. When marine plants began producing oxygen, it chemically combined with iron in solution to form oxides of iron such as hematite. The iron precipitated in vast amounts and was deposited along with sediments on shallow continental margins. Alternating bands of iron-rich and iron-poor sediments gave the ore a banded appearance, which is why it is named banded iron formation.

Much of the world's coal reserves are found in Paleozoic deposits (Figure 91). Extensive forests and swamps provided thick beds of peat that were buried under layers of sediments. The weight of the sediments and the Earth's internal heat reduced the peat to about one-twentieth of its original volume and transformed it in progressive stages into lignite, bituminous coal, and anthracite coal. Well-preserved, carbonized plant remains are commonly found between coal layers, indicating its vegetative origin.

A large portion of the world's oil reserves come from Paleozoic sediments, indicating a high degree of organic productivity in the ocean during this time. Marine organisms buried in shallow inland seas were covered by thick deposits of sediment. High temperatures and pressures "cooked" the organic compounds into oil, or natural gas if they were "overdone." The petroleum migrated into subterranean reservoirs composed of porous sandstone or limestone.

Extensive mountain-building activity, volcanism, and granitic intrusions in the late Paleozoic provided vein deposits of metallic ores. Important reserves of phosphate used for fertilizers were laid down in late Permian rocks in Idaho and adjacent states. Ore-bearing rocks of the Clinton iron formation, the chief iron producer in the Appalachian region from New York to Alabama, were precipitated by marine iron-eating bacteria.

Possibly the most important mineral resources for our modern industrialized world were deposited during the Mesozoic. Over half the known petroleum reserves are in Mesozoic sediments, and large quantities of oil

Figure 92   The Big Elk coal bed, King County, Washington. Photo 42 by J. D. Vine, courtesy USGS

and gas come from the Middle East, the Gulf Coast region, the Rockies, the North Slope of Alaska, and the North Sea. The great Mesozoic swamps produced thick coal deposits in the western United States (Figure 92) that rival those of the Carboniferous. Abundant deposits of coal are also found in Canada, South Africa, and Asia.

Porphyry copper deposits were formed in the cordilleran regions of North and South America. Triassic and Jurassic rocks in the western United States contained important reserves of uranium, which spurred the great uranium boom of the 1950s through the 1970s. The Mother Lode of the California gold rush days is late Jurassic or early Cretaceous in age. The diamond-bearing kimberlite pipes of South Africa are probably Cretaceous in age, although the diamonds they contain might have formed in the Archean.

Cenozoic mineral deposits include oil, natural gas, and coal in widely scattered parts of the world along with rich deposits of metallic minerals mostly in the Western Hemisphere. About half the world's oil fields are in Tertiary sediments, which contain nearly 40 percent of the world's oil reserves. Huge untapped reserves of oil are in oil-shale deposits in the

Figure 93 Oil shale deposit in the Green River Formation 8 miles west of Rangely, Colorado. Photo 293 by D. E. Winchester, courtesy USGS

western United States (Figure 93) with a potential oil content exceeding that of all other resources in the world.

Most of the metal-bearing ores of North and South America are thought to be products of Tertiary igneous activity. Important deposits of copper, lead, zinc, silver, and gold are found in the Rocky and Andes Mountain regions. A variety of other metallic deposits formed in the mountains of southern Europe during the Alpine orogeny and in the mountain ranges of southern Asia as well. Nonmetallic minerals such as sand and gravel, clay, salt, limestone, gypsum, and phosphates are mined in great quantities from Tertiary rocks the world over.

We have been blessed with a world rich in mineral wealth. When coal was united with steam in the mid-18th century, it ignited the Industrial Revolution, which transformed the face of the Earth. A serious by-product of this advancement, however, was pollution and the health hazards it entails. But generally, most industrial nations prospered in a manner that had been unprecedented in man's long climb up the ladder of progress. Unfortunately, the depletion of natural resources could threaten future advancement. The seemingly insatiable appetite for fossil fuels and ores to maintain a high standard of living in the industrialized world as well as to improve the standard of living in developing countries could very well lead to the depletion of known petroleum and high-grade ore reserves by the middle of the next century. After that, low-grade deposits would have to be worked, which could dramatically increase the cost of goods and commodities. Only through the conservation of natural resources will the wealth of the Earth be preserved for future generations.

8

GEMS AND PRECIOUS METALS

Gems, which are highly prized minerals, have a common appeal to all cultures, and their legacy extends back to prehistoric times. As far back as 20,000 years ago, our ancestors, the Cro-Magnon, lavished their bodies with strings of beads made from ivory, seashells, and gemstones. As is the custom today, the use of jewelry was determined by fashion and reflected one's rank in society. Gems were also thought to have mystical powers. Primitive cultures and even some modern people believe that gems and crystals have the ability to heal.

Growing in popularity along with the gemstones were the *precious* metals gold and silver, and much blood has been spilt down through the ages for the attainment of these commodities. The plundering of Inca gold and silver by the 16th-century Spaniards was largely responsible for the downfall of the greatest empire in South America. As poetic justice of a sort, the inflation of large amounts of Inca gold and silver into its economy eventually brought down the Spanish empire as well. The forty-niners' mad scramble for gold in California quickly swelled its population, gave the state a unique character, and allowed it to enter the Union much sooner than expected.

QUARTZ GEMS

The quartz gems are the best known among the semiprecious stones and produce a greater variety of gemstones than any other mineral. The transparent varieties possess a rainbow of colors from clear to yellow, blue, violet, green, pink, brown, and black. Rose quartz, named for the color of the rose flower, has a subtle shade of pink due to the presence of manganese. Smoky quartz obtained its brown color by the presence of small amounts of radioactive elements such as radium, which irradiated silicon atoms. Quartz cat's-eyes formed when quartz crystallized around preexisting minerals, sometimes altering them into unusual specimens. The translucent or opaque quartz gems, which are grouped under the name chalcedony, have a wide array of colors and forms, and some have a banded, striped, or mottled appearance.

Amethyst is the most valuable of the quartz gems, and until the 18th century it ranked among the most precious of stones. Amethyst contains iron that is finely dispersed throughout the crystal, giving it a spread of colors from orchid pink to regal purple: hues not seen elsewhere in the entire realm of gems. The stone was once believed to protect its wearer from drunkenness. (Of course, he had to abstain from alcohol for the protection to work.)

Opal is perhaps the most famous of the quartz gems and is renowned for its vivid flashes of colored light, typically red, orange, yellow, and green, colors no other gemstone possesses. Fire opal is so-named because of its flamelike colors. The play of colors in opal is derived by the diffraction of light rather than by absorption. The flashes can spread evenly across the gem's surface or become irregular points of light as the gem is rotated. The scintillations probably arise from the manner in which opal was deposited, involving layers of microscopic spherules of

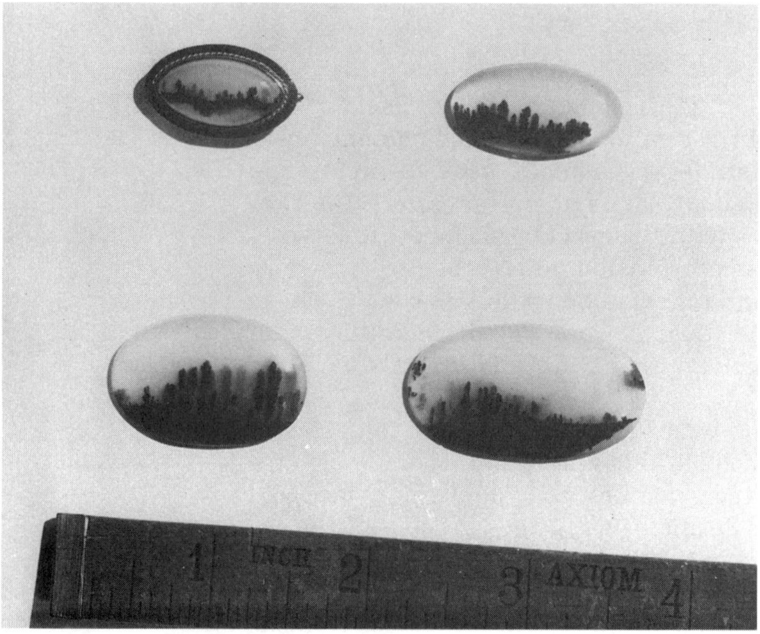

Figure 94 **Agates covered by moss-formed landscapes are found along the Yellowstone River and in adjacent regions of Montana.**
Photo 672 by D. B. Sterrett, courtesy USGS

hydrated silica that accumulated in thermal springs. Black opal from Nevada is found as a replacement mineral in fossil wood, seashells, and dinosaur bones.

Agate is known for its bands comprising alternating layers formed by intermittent deposits of silica from solution into irregular cavities in volcanic rocks. The concentric wavy patterns are derived from irregularities in the walls of the cavity. A number of varieties of agate are characterized by peculiarities in the shape and color of the bands. Moss agates, found along the Yellowstone River and adjacent regions, show magnificent landscapes (Figure 94). There are many legends concerning the healing power of agate, and it was once used to banish fear and protect against epilepsy.

Onyx is an agate with even, parallel bands usually colored black and white, brown and white, or red and white. It is largely used for making cameos (small sculptures carved on stones) because the design and background can be cut to appear in differently colored layers. The best cameos were produced by the ancients, and a revival of the art took place in the mid-19th century, when rich deposits of onyx were discovered in South America.

Jasper is closely related to agate and is composed of a large variety of chemical elements, which in turn give it various colors and designs. The colors range from red, yellow, brown, or any combination there of. Sometimes it is found banded with several different colored stripes. The ancients attributed many medicinal values to this stone, and even as late as the 17th century it was still believed that if jasper were hung around the neck it could cure stomach disorders.

Bloodstone, or heliotrope, was named the "gem that turns the sun" (*helio* meaning "sun"), and quantities of this stone were found near the ancient Egyptian city of Heliopolis. It is a dark green quartz with small spots of red jasper that resemble drops of blood. The gem was greatly prized in the Middle Ages and used for making sculptures representing violent death or martyrdom. Bloodstone was also believed to be capable of stopping hemorrhages and to possess the power of causing tempests.

TRANSPARENT GEMS

The transparent gems are known for their striking luster and brilliance along with their color and hardness. Most transparent gems are oxides of aluminum, beryllium, or magnesium with a few containing silica. Some transparent gems such as ruby and sapphire are identical in mineral composition and differ only in color. The value of these stones is determined largely by their transparency, lack of flaws, brilliance of color, and size.

Ruby is the most valued of all gemstones, and the deep red varieties are valued even more than diamonds. It is a vivid red gem of the mineral corundum, which is second in hardness to diamond on the Mohs hardness scale. The color varies from deep red to pale rose red, and in some stones it shows a tinge of violet. The oriental ruby, mined mostly in Burma, has very limited distribution, which accounts for its extraordinary high value. The ruby was considered by the Hindus as the king of the precious stones. It was also thought to bring fortune if the gem was worn on the left side of the body.

Sapphire is the serene blue variety of corundum and is essentially the same mineral as ruby, differing only in color and being slightly harder. It also comes in vivid green, violet, and yellow hues. The blue color of sapphire is attributed to the presence of oxides of chromium, iron, or titanium, The Montana variety has a peculiar electric blue color. Star sapphires are unusual in that they reflect light in a figure of a six-pointed star.

Emerald, known for its deep green color, is a gem of the mineral beryl and should not be confused with the oriental emerald, which is actually an emerald-colored sapphire. Colors vary from light green to dark green and are due to the presence of chromium. Compared to the other transparent gems, the emerald is relatively soft, only slightly harder than quartz. Emeralds were mined in Egypt as early as 1650 B.C., and Cleopatra's mines, located on the Red Sea coast east of Aswan, yielded precious emerald gems to adorn the queen of Egypt. Emeralds were once thought to have therapeutic value, curing such things as poisoning, diseases of the eye, and the possession of demons.

Zircon is one of the most extraordinary gems. A rich golden-brown variety is the most magnificent of all gemstones possessing this color. The natural colors range from clear varieties, which are favorite substitutes for diamonds, through shades of yellow and brown to deep brownish-red. Brown zircon crystals can be altered to a rich blue variety by heating them in the absence of air, which makes them more highly prized gems.

Tourmaline, often called the "rainbow gem," displays the widest range of exquisite colors of all the gems. Not only does it appear in almost every color of the rainbow, but a single tourmaline crystal might be half one color and half another or show three different colors like a candy cane. The profusion of colors is due to a complex chemical composition, involving perhaps a greater variety of chemical elements than any other mineral. The most valuable colors are a clear ruby red and a bright sapphire blue. Because of its unique crystal structure (Figure 95), tourmaline has a strange electrical property and becomes positively charged at one end and negatively charged at the other end of the crystal when heated. The static electricity will attract such objects as small bits of paper, similar to the way a comb drawn through the hair does.

Topaz is commonly a yellow gemstone but ranges in colors from pale yellow to brown. It has been very popular for jewelry from the 16th century onward. The rare pink topaz is much admired, especially the deeper hues. Topaz has a remarkably slick surface and a slippery feeling that distinguishes it from other minerals. Some large crystals, weighing upwards of 600 pounds, have been found in pegmatites. The mystical powers of topaz are believed to increase when the moon is new or full in the sign of Scorpio, at which time the wearer is thought to receive strong impressions from astral sources.

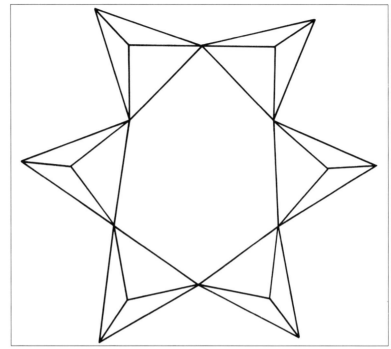

Figure 95   The structure of a tourmaline crystal.

OPAQUE GEMS

The opaque gems include representatives of metallic ores and rock-forming minerals, and with the exception of jade, they are used mainly as ornamental stones. Some opaque gems such as obsidian, a volcanic glass, and jet, an extremely hard form of coal, are better classified as rocks. (An unusual mineral that rightfully belongs to this group is the pearl because, as with all gems, it is highly prized for its beauty.)

Turquoise is a sky blue to bluish-green gemstone that has been used as an ornament since the dawn of civilization. Jewelry made from turquoise has been found in Egyptian and Sumerian tombs, dating back to the fourth millennium B.C. Because of its softness (slightly less than 6 on the Mohs hardness scale), turquoise was easy to work using the primitive tools available in ancient times. The demand for the gem in the United States has been high due to the popularity of turquoise jewelry made by native Americans in the West. For ages, the gem has been admired by the Navajos, who mined it long before the arrival of the Europeans. Most of the deposits

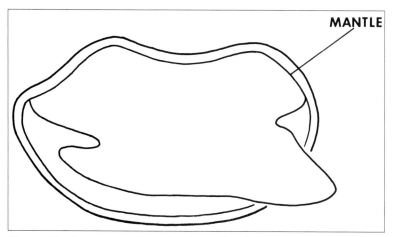

MANTLE

Figure 96   A cross section of a clam showing mantle area where a pearl often forms.

were in New Mexico, Arizona, Colorado, and Nevada. The mineral is associated with copper and occurs in nuggets or in veins. Sometimes tiny veins of clay and iron oxide crisscross the stone, giving it a much greater appeal.

Jade has been highly regarded since ancient times for its pleasant green color and versatility. It is a waxy or pearly mineral that is usually green but also possesses yellow, white, and pink colors. Jade comes in two varieties that are of different chemical composition but are similar in appearance. Jadeite is a pyroxene, and the light, translucent emerald green form is considered a precious stone. It is regarded as the more valuable of the two jades because it has a richer appearance and comes in a greater variety of colors. Nephrite is an amphibole and the more common of the two jades. Both varieties of jade have been carved into ornaments and implements since antiquity.

Moonstone, which is a variety of orthoclase called albite, is valued as a gemstone because of its bluish white or pearly opalescence. It receives its name from a moonlike silvery white sheen that changes on the surface as the light changes. Almost all moonstone of commercial value comes from mines in Sri Lanka (Ceylon) off the southern tip of India. It is said that knowledge of the future can be obtained by holding a moonstone in the mouth under a waning moon.

Malachite is a common ore of copper, and due to its conspicuous bright green color it is a useful guide for copper prospecting. It is often found together with azurite, which forms deep blue crystals, and the two minerals make a beautiful ornament when cut and polished. Malachite is also fashioned into urns, bowls, and a great variety of art objects. In the Middle Ages, malachite was especially treasured as a protection against the "evil eye."

Lapis lazuli (lazurite) has been in high favor as an ornamental stone for thousands of years. Deposits in a very remote part of Afghanistan were mined over 6000 years ago. It has an intense purplish blue color, which unlike many gems, does not fade in sunlight. The stone is used to make a variety of art objects and can be cut into a gemstone, although its softness does not make it entirely suitable for this purpose. Tradition holds that the Ten Commandments were inscribed on two blocks of this stone.

Pearl, known as the queen of gems, has been treasured by civilizations in all parts of the world for thousands of years. Even to this day, natural pearls are among the most prized of gemstones. Pearls are formed by a number of marine and freshwater mollusks such as clams and oysters when sand or some other particle irritates the animal's mantle that lines the inside of the shell (Figure 96). As a result, layers of aragonite grow year by year into a spherical concretion with a captivating iridescent luster. Pearls possess colors besides white, including hues of gold, pink, red, and black. The pearl was once esteemed as the emblem of purity, innocence, and peace.

DIAMONDS

The diamond is the most important of the gemstones, formed when carbon is subjected to high pressures and temperatures of the Earth's deep interior. A diamond's value depends on its hardness, its brilliance derived from a high index of refraction, or bending of light rays, and its "fire" derived from a strong dispersion of light. The value of a cut diamond depends on its color, purity, and size, as well as the skill with which it was cut. In general, the most valuable diamonds are those flawless stones that are colorless or possess a blue-white color. A faint straw-yellow color that diamonds often possess detracts from its value.

If diamonds are colored deep shades of yellow, red, green, or blue, they are called fancy stones and are greatly prized and bring very high prices. Diamonds can be colored deep shades of green by bombardment with nuclear radiation or blue by exposure to high-energy electrons. A stone colored green by irradiation can be heated to bring out a deep yellow hue. These artificially colored stones are difficult to distinguish from natural ones.

Diamonds have been discovered in many localities throughout the world, but only in a few places are they plentiful enough to be mined commercially. Most commonly, diamonds are found in alluvial or placer deposits derived from eroded volcanic mountains. They accumulate in these deposits because of their inert chemical nature, great hardness, and fairly high density. The earliest diamonds were mined from stream gravels in the southern and central portions of India. It is estimated that 12 million carats (the carat is a unit of weight for gemstones equal to 0.2 gram) were produced from Indian mines. India was virtually the only source of diamonds until they were discovered in Brazil in 1725. East-central Brazil produces about 160,000 carats annually, chiefly from stream gravels near the city of Diamantina, Minas Gerais.

Now about 95 percent of the world's output of diamonds comes from Africa. The Congo is by far the largest producer and supplies over 50 percent of the world's demand. The diamonds are mostly industrial grade, used for cutting tools, and represent only about 13 percent of the world's total value of diamonds produced. Industrial diamonds are also produced synthetically by subjecting pure carbon to extreme temperatures and pressures similar to those found deep inside the Earth. Several million carats are manufactured yearly, but these diamonds are not suitable for cutting into gemstones because of their small size.

Although some gem-quality diamonds are still recovered from gravels, the principal South African production is from kimberlite pipes (Figure 97), named for the town of Kimberley, South Africa. They are composed of jumbled fragments of mantle rocks, which are believed to have come from as deep as 150 miles below the surface. The intrusive bodies vary in size and shape, although many are roughly circular and pipe-shaped. Prospecting in South Africa for diamonds has uncovered over 700 kimberlite pipes and other intrusive bodies. However, most of these were found to be barren of diamonds.

The kimberlite deposits were originally worked as open pits, but as the mines became deeper,

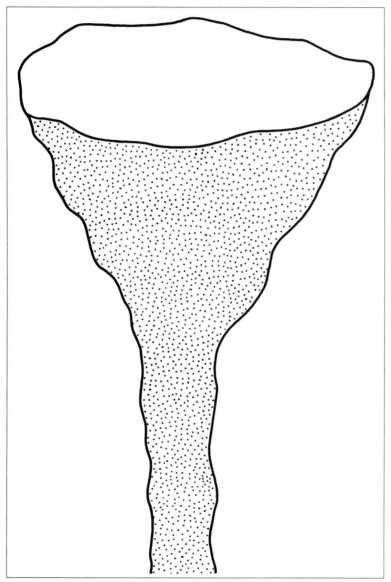

Figure 97   Kimberlite pipes are a major source of diamonds in South Africa.

underground methods had to be employed. At the Kimberley mine, the world's deepest diamond mine, the diameter of the pipe at the surface was about 1000 feet, and the width decreased sharply with depth. Mining stopped in 1908 at a depth of 3500 feet due to flooding, even though the pipe continued to greater depths. At the surface of the mine, the kimberlite is weathered to a soft yellow rock, and

Figure 98   The Saukville diamond (left) and Burlington diamond (right) found in Ozaukee and Racine Counties, Michigan, respectively.
Photo by W. F. Cannon, courtesy USGS

at deeper depths the rock grades into a harder "blue rock." The ratio of diamonds to barren rock was about 1 to 8 million by weight. The diamonds are extracted from the blue rock by first crushing it fine enough to permit concentration. This is spread out on tables coated with grease, to which the diamonds adhere while the waste material is washed away.

The world's largest and most productive diamond mine is the Premier mine, located 24 miles east of Pretoria, South Africa. Since mining began in 1903, over 30 million carats, or about 6 tons worth of diamonds, have been produced. The world's largest diamond, the Cullinan, weighing 3024 carats (21 ounces) was found there in 1905.

Diamonds have been found sparingly in other parts of the world, including Guyana, Venezuela, Australia, and various parts of the United States. Small stones have occasionally been discovered in stream sands along the eastern slope of the Appalachian Mountains from Virginia to Georgia. Diamonds have been reported from the gold sands of northern California and southern Oregon. Sporadic occurrences have also been found in glacial till deposits from Ohio, Wisconsin, and Michigan (Figure 98).

In 1906, diamonds were discovered in a kimberlite pipe near Murfreesboro, Arkansas. This locality resembled areas containing diamond pipes in South Africa, and was the site of the only operating diamond mine in the United States (Figure 99), yielding a total of about 40,000 stones. It is now a tourist attraction, known as the Crater of Diamonds State Park, where people pay a small fee to sift through the black soil in search of instant wealth. The diamond field is plowed regularly, and, generally, after a rainstorm is the best time to search for diamonds because the surface of the freshly turned soil is washed, exposing the diamonds, which might otherwise look like bits of glass.

Figure 99   The Arkansas diamond mine south of Murfreesboro, Arkansas, in 1923. A dragline scraper was used to mine diamond-bearing material.   Photo by H. D. Miser, courtesy USGS

GOLD AND SILVER

For more than 6000 years, man has adored and fought over gold, and this metal was responsible in part for the making of civilization. Gold is the universally accepted medium of exchange, and many nations fortunate enough to possess their own gold mines have little difficulty paying their debts. Gold is also a status symbol, and down through the ages people have adorned their bodies with this metal. Along with diamonds, gold is exchanged during marriage ceremonies in most parts of the world. Gold is even believed to have healing powers. People in Japan seek its medicinal powers by bathing in a tub fashioned into a shape of a phoenix made from 400 pounds of pure gold.

Gold does not tarnish and resists corrosion; gold coins recovered from sunken treasure ships that have laid on the bottom for centuries look as bright as new. Gold is extremely malleable, and a single ounce can be beaten into a sheet covering nearly 100 square feet. Visitors to Bangkok, Thailand, are often awestruck by the apparent abundance of gold spread on the rooftops of temples and other buildings until they realize how extremely thin gold gilding can be made. Even glass coated with a thin film of gold can reflect the summer's sun and retain a building's heat during the winter (which can bring about a substantial saving in utility costs!).

The California gold rush began in early 1848 with the discovery of gold at John Sutter's sawmill near present-day Sacramento. Word spread like wildfire, and soon Californians headed for the hills to mine gold. They were soon joined by get-rich-quick men from other parts of the country, who stormed into California from all directions. Several thousand poorly equipped fortune hunters died along the way, mostly from disease, famine, and cold. Mining camps sprang into shantytowns, where miners lived under primitive conditions, and claim disputes and drunken brawls were common occurrences. Supplies had to be paid for in gold dust, and prices were outrageous. Out of the many thousands who went into the mountains to dig for gold, only a few actually got rich; most of whom did so by mining the pockets of other miners.

Figure 100   Alluvial fans from the Sierra Nevada Range, Death Valley National Monument. Photo 455 by H. E. Malde, courtesy USGS

The gold-bearing veins of the foothills of the western Sierra Nevada Range in California (Figure 100) are usually steeply inclined ledges dipping into the granite roots of the mountains. The hydrothermal veins of the Mother Lode system trend north-south, covering a distance of some 200 miles. The veins are composed of a hard, milky-white quartz, generally no more than 3 feet wide. The quartz might have a few specks of gold and pyrite (fool's gold) sprinkled throughout, but seldom did stringers of pure gold shoot through the veins. Most miners panned for gold out of the sand and gravels that washed down from the mountains.

Gold has a specific gravity or density of about 19, making it roughly eight times heavier than ordinary sands and gravels. Therefore, if gold sands are placed in suspension with water by vigorous swirling or sluicing, the gold will fall out of the mixture and end up on the bottom of a gold pan or sluice box. This technique is known as placer mining (Figure 101), and for this type of mine to be profitable many tons of sand and gravel, along with large quantities of water, had to be processed. An individual panning for gold will most likely not get rich, but at the present price of around $400 a troy ounce (12 ounces per pound) he or she might possibly find enough to pay for provisions with a little left over. The forty-niners rarely did so.

Figure 101 Placer gold mining in Borens Gulch, La Plata County, Colorado, in 1875. Photo by W. H. Jackson, courtesy USGS

The gold rush did not stop in California but headed eastward into Nevada, Wyoming, Colorado, and New Mexico. Perhaps, the most colorful mining episodes and mines with the most colorful names were located in the Colorado Mountains (Figure 101a), which are peppered with old abandoned mining camps. When the underground mines played out, gold-dredging techniques were developed (Figure 102). Some of the old mining towns eventually became ski resorts and tourist attractions, while many more became ghost towns with only a few remnants to mark the past.

Silver is often associated with gold, and the Comstock Lode in Nevada was the scene of one of the largest mining booms in the history of the opening of the American West. Originally discovered in 1859, pro-

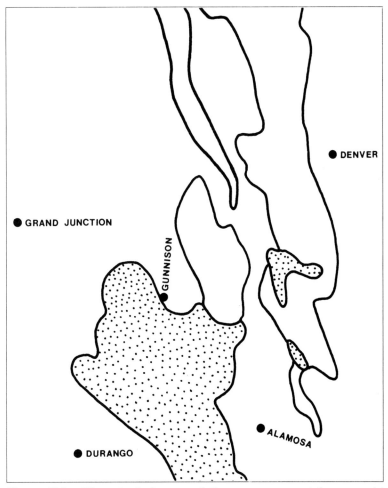

Figure 101a   The stippled areas of the map represent former gold mining districts in Colorado.

duction did not reach its peak until the 1870s. Many mines were scattered along a 3-mile mineralized fault zone that separated young volcanic rocks from older rocks. The lode forms a slab, inclined about 40 degrees to the horizontal, and reaches a thickness of 400 feet and a depth of 3000 feet below the surface. The silver combines with sulfur to make simple silver minerals such as argentite, with a nearly 3 percent gold content, which helped make mining more profitable.

The gold and silver mines in South America were responsible in large part for the Spanish settlement there shortly after Columbus discovered America. Natives of the Inca Empire, which stretched halfway down the

Figure 102   A gold dredge on Lay Creek, Colorado. Photo by H. S. Gale, courtesy USGS

Andes Mountains, extending some 3000 miles from Columbia to Argentina, mined gold and silver out of eroded stumps of ancient volcanoes. Cerro Rico (hill of silver) is a 15,000-foot volcano (Figure 103) that was literally shot through with veins of silver.

When the Spanish conquistadors first landed in Peru in 1532, they found the Inca Empire torn by civil war. The Spaniards had little difficulty taking over the Empire, and captured a great deal of gold and silver along with the masterpieces of Inca goldsmiths, which they melted into bullion, and sent the treasure on to Spain. Some Spanish galleons, heavily loaded with gold and silver, were lost during storms at sea, and today, their precious cargoes are eagerly sought after by undersea treasure hunters.

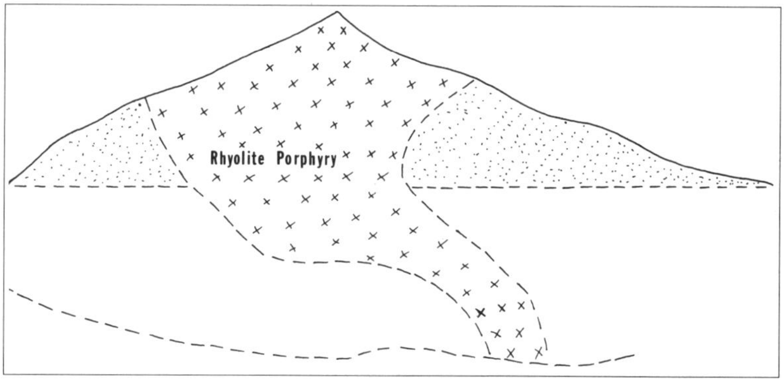

Rhyolite Porphyry

Figure 103   A cross section through the Cerro Rico silver mine, Bolivia, showing the rhyolite porphyry.

9

THE RARE AND UNUSUAL

Every once in a while, someone makes a momentous discovery, which defies our preconceived notions about the "real world." Physicists study the microworld and believe that by breaking atoms into tiny little pieces they can tell us something about the origin of the universe. Geologists study the macroworld in search of clues about how the Earth originated. Astronomers study the megaworld and look to the stars to tell us something about our galaxy and the vast expanse that lies beyond.

Meanwhile, there are plenty of unsolved riddles down here on Earth. For instance, what was the purpose of the megaliths at Stonehenge in southern England? Was the volcanic island of Thera, which exploded in 1580 B.C., really the fabled continent of Atlantis? How did Ayers Rock, the largest rock in the world, measuring 5.5 miles long and 1100 feet high, happen to get in the middle of the desert in central Australia? The rocks will ultimately help solve some of our most puzzling questions and might someday tell us why the dinosaurs disappeared.

ROCKS THAT FOLLOW THE SUN

Hundreds of millions of years ago, single-celled organisms recorded in rock the interactions of the sun, Earth, and moon. These organisms built stromatolite structures, composed of concentric layers of sediment that tilted in the average direction of the sun. Stromatolites found in the Bitter Springs Formation in central Australia provided an 850-million-year-old fossil record of the sun's movement across the sky. If a stromatolite were situated near the equator, it pointed south in the winter and north in the summer and developed a growth pattern in the shape of a sine wave (Figure 104).

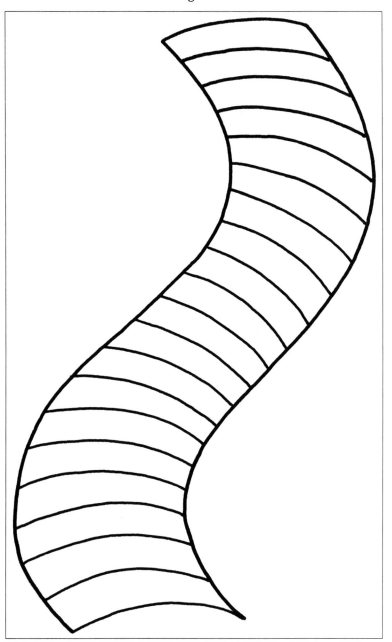

Figure 104 Stromatolites developed a growth pattern in the shape of a sine wave, which depicted the number of days in a year.

If new sediment layers were constructed each day, then the number of layers appearing in one wavelength represented the number of days in a year during the time of the stromatolite's growth. Thus, from stromatolites living in the late Proterozoic we can estimate that there were 435 days in a single year. The results agree well with counting the growth rings of ancient coral fossils to estimate the number of days in a year as far back as the beginning of the Cambrian period, 570 million years ago.

In addition, the sine-wave patterns of ancient stromatolites contain information about the maximum travel of the sun across the equator. The equator forms an oblique angle to the plane of the Earth's orbit around the sun, called the ecliptic. This angle is controlled by the tilt of the Earth's rotational axis. The maximum latitude of the sun during the peak of each season is obtained by measuring the maximum angle at which the sine wave deviates from the average direction of stromatolite growth. Today, the sun travels 23.5 degrees north of the equator during the summer and 23.5 degrees south of the equator during the winter. However, about 850 million years ago, this value was about 26.5 degrees, which indicates

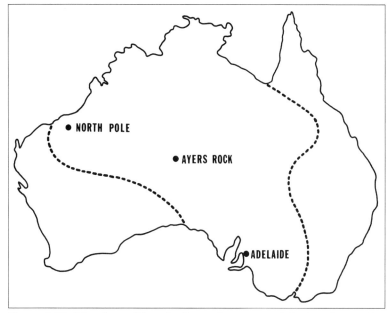

Figure 105   The dotted lines indicate the extent of the late Precambrian Ice Age in Australia.

that the climate at that time would have been much more seasonal than it is today.

Present-day stromatolites live in the intertidal zones, above the low tide mark and their height is indicative of the height of the tides, which is mostly controlled by the gravitational pull of the moon. The stromatolite colonies of the Warrawoona group in North Pole, Western Australia, at 3.5-billion-years, the oldest on Earth, grew to tremendous heights with some over 30 feet tall. This suggests that at an early age the moon was much closer to the Earth, and because of its stronger gravitational attraction at this range it raised tremendous tides that must have flooded coastal areas several miles inland.

This also explains why the length of day was so much shorter. The early Earth rotated much faster than it does today, and as it slowed its rotational rate due to drag forces produced by the tides, it transferred some of its angular momentum (rotational energy) to the moon, flinging it out into a wider orbit. Even today, the moon is receding from the Earth at a rate of about 2 inches per year.

The solar cycle is a periodic fluctuation of solar output, occurring today about every 22 years. Evidence for a solar cycle operating as far back as the Precambrian is thought to exist in 680-million-year-old glacial varves, or banded deposits, found in lake bed sediments north of Adelaide in South

Figure 106   Australian desert varves composed of cyclic laminations of sandstones and siltstones.

Australia. The varves consist of alternating layers of silt laid down annually during the late Precambrian ice age (Figure 105). Each summer when the glacial ice melted, meltwater loaded with sediment discharged into a lake below the glacier, and the sediments settled out to form a stratified deposit (Figure 106). During times of intense solar activity, the Earth's climatic temperature increased slightly, causing more glacial melting and the deposition of thicker varves. By counting the layers of thick and thin varves, we can establish a stratigraphic sequence that mimics both the 11-year sunspot cycle, the occurrence of large numbers of sunspots on the sun's surface, and the 22-year solar cycle or possibly the early lunar cycle, covering the full range of lunar orbital motions, which today is about 19 years.

Another type of stratified deposit that could well be the most beautiful, valuable, and enigmatic rock ever created on the planet are the banded iron formations. Composed of alternating layers of iron and silica, they were formed about 2 billion years ago at the height of the earliest ice age. For unknown reasons, major episodes of iron deposition coincided with periods of glaciation. It is also believed that on average the oceans were much warmer at that time than they are at present. When iron- and silicate-rich warm currents flowed toward the glaciated polar regions, the suddenly cooled waters could no longer hold the minerals in solution. They thus precipitated out, forming alternating layers due to difference in settling rates between silica and iron, the heavier of the two minerals.

MINERALS THAT REVERSE THEMSELVES

Over the last 170 million years, for still unexplained reasons, the Earth's magnetic field has reversed polarity some 300 times, for the last time about 730,000 years ago. During a reversal, the Earth temporarily lets down its magnetic shield, which protects it from cosmic radiation. Proof that the Earth's magnetic poles periodically change places is found on the ocean floor near spreading centers, where new oceanic crust is being generated. As layers of basalt cool, they become slightly magnetized and acquire the polarity of the magnetic poles at the time of their deposition. In addition, one set of alternating magnetic bands of basalt is the mirror image of the opposite set on the other side of the spreading ridge (Figure 107). This property became the clinching proof for seafloor spreading because in order for the magnetic strips to form in such a manner the seafloor had to be spreading apart.

Magnetite, which faithfully records the Earth's magnetic field, was thought to be the dominant magnetic mineral in rocks. But in the early 1950s, a rare mineral called titanohematite was found to have the odd ability to become magnetized in the opposite direction of the Earth's magnetic field. This unusual behavior could have played havoc with scientists trying to prove the theory of magnetic pole reversal. Their existence could also complicate the analysis of the magnetic orientations in rocks used to date lava flows.

Although once thought to be exceedingly rare, self-reversing minerals more recently have been found in sedimentary basins and lava fields of

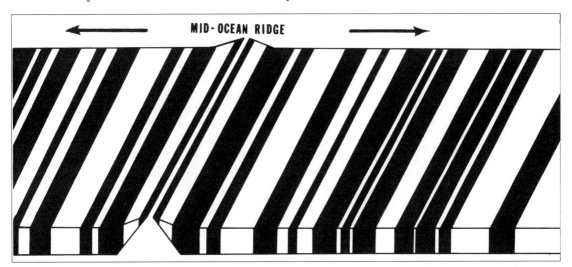

Figure 107   Magnetic stripes on the ocean floor are mirror images of each other and indicate that the ocean crust is spreading apart.

Figure 108 A map indicating the location of self-reversing minerals in the western United States.

western North America (Figure 108), where, in some places, they are the dominant magnetic minerals. For example, relatively abundant titano-hematites were found in 10,000-year-old lava flows of California's Mount Shasta Volcano (Figure 109).

Normally, when rocks are imprinted with a magnetic field, the magnetic fields of their atoms line up with the Earth's magnetic field as they cool past their Curie point, the temperature at which a magnetic field becomes

Figure 109 Mount Shasta in the Cascade Range, Siskiyou County, California. Photo by C. D. Miller, courtesy USGS

134

permanent. Below that point, the field freezes until the rock is reheated, which destroys the magnetic field. Thus, the magnetic fields can be thought of as tiny fossil compasses, pointing in whatever direction the Earth's magnetic field happened to be during deposition. Self-reversing minerals, however, have two Curie points, one occurring at a higher temperature than the other. As the mineral cools, it develops two magnetic regions: the first with its magnetic field aligned with the Earth's, and the second with a much stronger field aligned in the opposite direction. Thus, the final polarity of the rock's magnetic field is reversed.

HALOS OF STONE

In the permafrost regions of the Arctic, soil and rocks are fashioned into strikingly beautiful and orderly patterns that have confronted geologists for centuries. Every summer, the retreating snows unveil a bizarre assortment of rocks arranged in a honeycomblike network as the ground begins to thaw, giving the landscape the appearance of a tiled floor. These patterns are found in most of the northern lands and alpine regions, where the soil is exposed to moisture and seasonal freezing and thawing. The polygons range in size from a few inches across when composed of small pebbles to several tens of feet when large boulders form protective rings around mounds of soil (Figure 110).

The polygons were probably produced by forces similar to those that cause frost heaving, which pushes rocks up through the soil. (This phenomenon is well known to northern farmers, as every spring brings a new crop of stones to their fields.) The boulders move through the soil either by a pull from above or by a push from below. If the top of the rock freezes first, it is pulled up by the expanding frozen soil.

Figure 110   Stone polygons east of Maclaren River, Clearwater Mountains, Valdex Creek District, Alaska. Note the complete sorting between the clay-rich centers and the bordering lines of coarse boulders. Photo by C. Wahrhaftig, courtesy USGS

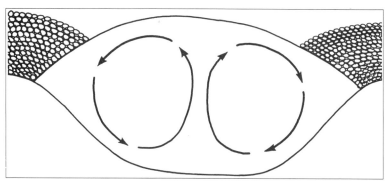

Figure 111 The formation of polygonal structures by connective cells, which bring coarser material to the surface.

Figure 112 A pattern of scalloped cracks near Stovepipe Wells, Death Valley National Monument, California. Photo courtesy National Park Service

When the soil thaws, the rock settles down at a slightly higher level. The expanding frozen soil lying below could also heave the rock upward. After several freeze-thaw cycles, the boulder finally rests on the surface.

The regular polygonal-patterned ground might have been formed by the movement of soil of mixed composition upward toward the center of the mound and downward under the boulders. The soil might move in convective cells (Figure 111). The coarser material composed of gravel and boulders is gradually shoved radially outward from the central area, leaving the finer materials behind. This idea is supported by the fact that the material in the center of the mound often appears churned up. Rocks also have been known to push their way through highway pavement, and fenceposts have been known to be shoved completely out of the ground by frost heaving.

Other examples of patterned ground include polygonal shapes created in desert muds (Figure 112), which were formed by the contraction of the mud when it dried rapidly in the hot sun. Sorted circles might also form by the increased wearing down of coarse grains in isolated cracks in bedrock. Even vibrations from earthquakes are thought to cause the sorting of some sediments. There are also curious occurrences of patterns that form in sediments on the ocean floor.

WHISTLING STONES

If a volcano erupts explosively and casts fluid lava high into the air, the lava disperses by the wind, giving rise to particles of various sizes from ash to molten blobs of lava up to 15 feet wide, called volcanic bombs (Figure 113). Often volcanic bombs are still soft enough to change shape during their flight through the air and tend to flatten or splatter when they land. If they cool in flight, volcanic bombs form a variety of shapes. The various

Figure 113   Volcanic bombs at the southwest base of a cinder cone, 10 miles northwest of Lassen Peak, Cascade Range, Shasta County, California. Photo by J. S. Diller, courtesy USGS

types of volcanic bombs go under the names cannonball, spindle, breadcrust, cow dung, ribbon, or fusiform, depending on their shape or surface appearance. Bread-crust bombs, which often reach several feet across, are also named for their crusty appearance, caused by gases escaping from the bomb while the outer surface is hardening. Sometimes volcanic bombs actually explode when they hit the ground due to the rapid expansion of gas in the molten interior when the solid crust cracks open on impact. Often, volcanic bombs spin wildly through the air, and this causes them to whistle like incoming cannon fire.

MINERALS THAT GLOW IN THE DARK

When rays from an ultraviolet lamp called a black light strike certain minerals, their atoms become excited (rapidly vibrate) and reradiate energy at a lower wavelength, often providing strikingly brilliant colors. This effect is termed *fluorescence*, named after the mineral fluorite, which often glows blue violet when a black light is shown on it. The overwhelming majority of fluorescent minerals are not very impressive until a black light is turned on them, when the ultraviolet rays produce vivid and intense colors. Fluorescent minerals usually contain a small amount of impurities, such as manganese, which are called activators. These enhance a mineral's ability to glow in the presence of ultraviolet rays. If a mineral continues to glow for a short time (up to several minutes) after the ultraviolet light source has been removed, it is *phosphorescent*. These minerals are much less common than those that fluoresce. In addition, some minerals only fluoresce in shortwave ultraviolet, whereas others only fluoresce in long-wave ultraviolet. However, many fluorescent minerals glow in both ultraviolet wavelengths. Therefore, when exploring for fluorescent minerals, it is advisable to select a black light that uses both ultraviolet wavelengths.

Willemite, a zinc ore, was first discovered to have fluorescent properties at the Franklin mine in New Jersey, where spectacular fluorescent specimens are perhaps the finest in the world. Miners observed a brilliant green glow from Willemite when they exposed it to the ultraviolet rays of an arc lamp in a dark mine shaft. Franklin calcite also fluoresces, providing a brilliant red color.

Scheelite, the most important tungsten ore in North America, is one of the few minerals that always fluoresce. Geologists explore for scheelite by shining a black light on suspected outcrops at night and look for a characteristic blue glow. If the mineral glows yellow, molybdenum, an important mineral for hardening steel, is present. Scapolite, a complex silicate metamorphic mineral, glows an appealing yellow under a black light. Opal from the western states glows green due to a small amount of uranium impurities present. Uranium ores, besides being detected by their radioactivity, pro-

Figure 114　A large lightning bolt. Photo courtesy National Oceanic and Atmospheric Administration (NOAA)

duce strikingly beautiful hues of yellow and green under ultraviolet light. Even diamonds will fluoresce under a black light with various hues of blue.

LIGHTNING-FAST GLASS

A few years ago, two boys stumbled upon an unusual rock near Winans Lake, Michigan, that was thought to be a huge dinosaur leg bone. Scientists from the Museum of Paleontology at the University of Michigan went out to investigate, only to find that the 15-foot-long white, green, and gray object was the world's largest fulgurite, a tube-shaped glob of glass that formed when a powerful lightning bolt struck the ground (Figure 114).

For centuries, scientists have known that large lightning bolts, which can attain temperatures several times those on the surface of the sun, can melt or vaporize rocks they strike. However, until recently, the chemical and physical processes behind the formation of fulgurites was largely unknown. In addition, the studies revealed the presence of two metallic

Figure 115   The Wolf Creek meteorite from Western Australia, showing crack development on cut surface. Photo 6 by G. T. Faust, courtesy USGS

minerals that had never before been found to occur in nature. Electron microscope analysis of metallic globules found embedded in the fulgurite glass also showed them to be composed of a variety of iron and silicon metal compounds previously known only to exist in meteorites. Apparently, the lightning bolt somehow chemically reduced (removed the oxygen from) the original iron oxides in the ground, even reducing the metals to a greater extent than those found in most meteorites. The fulgurite was also enriched in gold, which the lightning apparently scavenged from the surrounding soil and concentrated in the glass.

STONES FROM THE SKY

The origin of meteorites, which are metallic or stony bodies that enter the Earth's atmosphere and impact on the ground (Figure 115) has been a long-standing puzzle. The most accepted theory is that they come from the asteroid belt lying between Mars and Jupiter. Certain rare meteorites might also be pieces of Martian crust blasted out by large meteorite impacts. The asteroid belt contains bodies ranging in size from small grains called micrometeorites to chunks of rock that can be hundreds of miles wide called asteroids.

No one has yet been able to explain how these rock fragments managed to get into orbits that cross our planet's path. Apparently, the asteroids behave themselves fairly well and run in nearly circular orbits around the sun for as long as a million years or more. Then, for unknown reasons, possibly due to the gravitational attraction of a passing comet or the pull of Jupiter's gravity, their orbits suddenly stretch to become so elliptical that some of them strike the Earth.

Meteorite falls are more common than most people realize. Every day thousands of meteorites rain down on the Earth, and occasional meteor showers can involve hundreds of thousands of stones. More than 1 million tons of meteoritic material is produced annually. Most meteors completely burn up on entering the atmosphere, and their ashes contribute to the load of atmospheric dust, which is largely responsible for our blue skies and red sunsets. The remainder that make it through the atmosphere can cause havoc, as numerous examples of meteorites crashing into houses can attest to.

The majority of meteorites have been found by farmers plowing their fields. Surprisingly, one of the best places for meteorite hunting is in Antarctica, where the dark meteorites lie on the surface in stark contrast to the glacial ice, making them easy to spot. The largest known meteorite, named the Hoba West, was found in 1920 near Grootfontein in South-West Africa and weighed about 60 tons. One of the largest meteorites actually seen to fall was an 880-pound stone that landed in a farmer's field near Paragould, Arkansas, on March 27, 1886.

Figure 116   The Manicouagan impact structure, Quebec, Canada. Photo courtesy NASA

In addition to the metallic and stone meteorites, a great deal of carbon falls out of the sky, as though tons of coal were raining from the heavens. These fragments are primitive meteorites called carbonaceous chondrites, which are chunks of carbon-rich rock with small spherical mineral inclusions called chondrules and are possibly leftovers from the formation of the Solar System 4.6 billion years ago. Amino acids and DNA bases, indicating the precursors of life, have been found in meteorites that formed elsewhere in the Solar System. The billion-year-old Murchison meteorite found in Australia in 1969 contains lipidlike organic compounds that were able to self-assemble into cellular membranes, an essential requirement for the first living cells.

Currently, numerous large circular structures are spread around the world, which could have resulted from substantial meteorite impacts. The New Quebec Crater in northern Canada is 2 miles in diameter, 1300 feet deep, and filled with water. One of the largest impact structures is outlined

Figure 117   Meteor Crater near Winslow, Arizona. Photo 352, courtesy USGS

by the distinctively circular Manicouagan reservoir (Figure 116) in east-central Quebec, which is nearly 60 miles in diameter. The best-preserved meteorite impact crater is Meteor Crater (Figure 117) in the Arizona desert near Winslow, which measures nearly a mile across and several hundred feet deep. It was gouged out roughly 22,000 years ago by a meteorite weighing over 60,000 tons.

When a large meteorite slams into the Earth, it kicks up a great deal of sediment. The finer material is lofted high into the atmosphere, while the coarse debris falls back around the perimeter of the crater, forming a high, steep-banked rim. Not only are the rocks shattered in the vicinity of the impact, but the shock wave also causes shock metamorphism of the surrounding rocks, changing their composition and crystal structure. The force of the impact also fuses sediment into small, dark glassy spheres called tektites.

In South Africa, researchers found extensive deposits of these spherules over 1 foot thick, which dated to 3.5 billion years. In addition, spherules of Archean age have been found in Australia. The spherules resemble chondrules, found on carbonaceous chondrites and in lunar soils. The discoveries might support the idea that massive meteorite bombardments during the Archean played a major role in shaping the surface of the Earth and providing it with the necessary ingredients for life. It has also been suggested that a very large meteorite might have triggered the process of plate tectonics by cracking the Earth's crust into several plates.

Another consequence of large meteorite impacts are shocked quartz grains that are characterized by prominent striations across crystal faces. Minerals such as quartz and feldspar develop these features when high-pressure shock waves exert shearing forces on the crystals, producing parallel fracture planes called lamellae. The presence of shocked quartz in sedimentary deposits at the Cretaceous-Tertiary (K-T) boundary all around the world is used as evidence that the Earth was struck by one or more large meteorites, injecting huge amounts of debris into the upper atmosphere and setting global-wide forest fires, which in turn sent large amounts of soot into the lower atmosphere. Such a fire was set in a forest near Vanavara in central Soviet Asia in 1908 by an exploding comet that devastated trees for several hundred square miles as though they were hit by a multimegaton hydrogen bomb. An impact of this size is expected to occur at least once every century.

The pall of dust and smoke from a large meteorite impact could block out the sun and place the Earth in a deep freeze. This might possibly account for the disappearance of the dinosaurs and three-quarters of all known species 65 million years ago. Very powerful volcanoes also produce shocked quartz grains called shards, which are used to support the volcanistic theory for the extinctions at the end of the Cretaceous.

However, these shocked quartz grains have only single sets of lamellae rather than the multiple lamellae seen in quartz from the K-T boundary as well as from meteorite impact sites. In addition, 25 percent of the quartz at the K-T boundary sites is shocked, whereas less than 1 percent of the quartz is shocked at the Toba Volcano in Indonesia, which erupted 75,000 years ago and is believed to be the greatest explosive eruption in the last 2 million years. This seems to preclude the possibility that volcanoes alone played any significant role in the extinction event. However, both a large meteorite impact and a period of increased volcanism, possibly brought on by such an impact, might better explain the decline in species, caused by a dramatic change in climate. This has important implications, for should the Earth again be struck by a large meteorite the environmental consequences might be too harsh for most species to survive, causing another mass extinction, which seems to be a normal occurrence for life on this planet.

10

WHERE FOSSILS AND MINERALS ARE FOUND

Fossils and rock specimens can be found by the amateur nearly everywhere. The vast majority of fossils are located in ancient marine sediments, some of which accumulated when inland seas invaded the continents during times of rising sea levels. Most minerals found in sedimentary rocks were precipitated from seawater. When land is eroded, some 3 billion tons of rock are dissolved by water and carried by streams to the sea each year. This is sufficient to lower the entire land surface of the Earth by an inch in 2000 years. It is also one of the reasons why the ocean is so salty. Besides ordinary table salt, seawater contains large amounts of calcium carbonate, calcium sulfate, and silica. These minerals precipitate from seawater by biologic or chemical processes. They also can replace other minerals or the skeletal remains in fossils.

Many fossils can be found in abandoned limestone quarries and gravel pits, where the rocks are well exposed and conveniently broken up. Also, abundant fossil plant leaves and stems can be found in abandoned coal pits. Because many old abandoned ore mines are excavated in igneous rocks, in which most minerals are found, these places as well as other granitic outcrops are often excellent sites for finding minerals with good

Figure 118 **Undercut sea cliff of Pleistocene coral limestone at Port Denison, Western Australia. The maximum depth of the notch corresponds approximately to the mean sea level.** Photo 10 by R. W. Fairbridge, courtesy USGS

crystals. In addition to these, rock outcrops, road cuts, stream beds, and sea cliffs (Figure 118) offer good rock exposures for collecting fossils and minerals.

FOSSIL-BEARING ROCKS

In areas where marine sediments outcrop, chances are good that these sediments are fossiliferous, meaning they contain abundant fossils. Indeed, few places in this country have no fossils, because most parts of the North American continent have been invaded by seas at various times, allowing marine sediments to accumulate. Even the presently high interior of the continent was once invaded by inland seas (Figure 119), and thick marine sediments were deposited in the deep basins. When the seas departed and the land rose higher, erosion exposed many of these marine sediments along with their content of fossils.

Limestones are among the best rocks for finding fossils. This is due to their sedimentation, incorporating shells and skeletons of dead marine life that were buried and fused into solid rock. Most limestones are marine in origin with some deposits originating in lakes. Limestones constitute approximately 10 percent of all exposed sedimentary rocks. Shales are the most prominate sediments, followed by sandstones.

Many limestones form massive outcrops (Figure 120), which are recognized by their typically light gray or light brown colors. The application of a few drops of 10 percent hydrochloric acid solution (available at drug stores and rock shops) is a further test for limestone. The reaction of acid on calcium carbonate produces a strong effervescence on a fresh surface. This is also a good test for limey mudstones and sandstones because they are cemented with calcite.

Whole or partial fossils constitute most limestones, depending on whether they were deposited in quiet or agitated waters. Tiny spherical grains called oolites are characteristic of agitated water, whereas lithified layers of limey mud called micrite are characteristic of calm waters. In quiet waters, undisturbed by waves and currents, whole organisms with hard body parts are buried in calcium carbonate sediments, which are later lithified into limestone. In agitated waters near shore, shells and other hard body parts are fragmented by the back-and-forth motion of the waves and tides.

Most carbonate sediments were deposited in

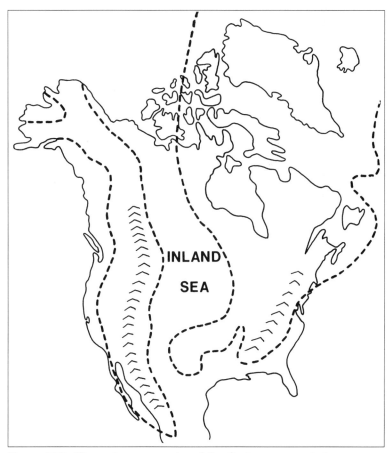

Figure 119   The paleogeography of the Cretaceous period.

fairly shallow waters, probably less than 50 feet deep, and the majority of these were deposited in intertidal zones, where marine organisms are plentiful. Coral reefs, which form in shallow water, where sunlight can easily penetrate, contain abundant organic remains. Many ancient carbonate reefs are composed largely of carbonate mud with larger skeletal remains literally "floating" in the mud.

Some carbonate rocks were deposited in deep seas; however, their fossil content is usually poor. The maximum depth carbonate rocks can form is controlled by the calcium carbonate compensation zone, which generally begins about 2 miles deep. Below this depth, the cold, high-pressure waters of the abyssal, which contain the vast majority of free carbon dioxide, dissolves calcium carbonate that sinks to this level.

Carbonate rocks began as sandy or muddy calcium carbonate material. The sand-size particles are composed of broken-up skeletal remains of invertebrates and shells of calcareous algae that rain from above. Skeletal

Figure 120   Limestone formation of the Bend group in a ravine at the base of the Sierra Diablo escarpment, Culberson County, Texas. Photo 284 by P. B. King, courtesy USGS

remains might have been broken by mechanical means, such as the pounding of the surf, or by the activity of living organisms. Further breakdown into dust-size particles produces a carbonate mud (sometimes called marl), which is the most common constituent of carbonate rocks.

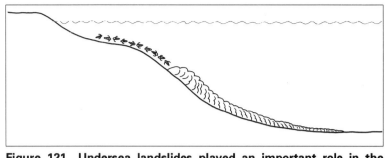

Figure 121 Undersea landslides played an important role in the fossilization of species.

Under certain conditions, carbonate mud might dissolve in seawater and redeposit elsewhere on the ocean floor as calcite ooze. If dissolved calcium carbonate is deposited around a small nucleus such as a skeletal fragment or a quartz grain, it grows by adding layers of concentric rings into a sand-size particle called an oolith.

As calcareous sediments accumulate into thick deposits on the ocean floor, deep burial of the lower strata produces high pressures, which lithifies them into carbonate rock, consisting mostly of limestone or dolostone. If fine-grained calcareous sediments are not strongly lithified, they form deposits of soft, porous chalk. If the sediments consist mostly of fragments of skeletal remains, they are cemented into a limestone called coquina. Limestones typically develop a secondary crystalline texture, whereby crystals grow after formation of the original rock by solution and recrystallization. Fossils in the limestone also recrystallize and are often destroyed by this process.

Shales and mudstones commonly contain fossils and are the most abundant sedimentary rocks on Earth, because they are the main weathering products of feldspars, which are the most abundant minerals. In addition, all rocks are eventually ground to clay-size particles by abrasion. Because clay particles are so small and sink slowly, they normally settle out in calm, deep waters far from shore. Compaction squeezes out the water between sediment grains, and the clay is lithified into shale, which is easy to recognize by its thin, fissile (easily split) layers. Organisms caught in the clay are compressed into thin carbonized remains or impressions.

The deep, calm bottom waters were probably stagnant and oxygen poor. Periodic slumping from a high bank would result in a flow of mud into the deeper waters. Organisms living on or in the shallow muddy bottom are caught in the slide and buried in the mud when the slide came to a halt in deeper water (Figure 121). Because scavengers cannot survive in these waters, the remains of the organisms were favored for preservation. As the

Figure 122   A large fossil leaf in a sandstone block found at the Coryell coal mines, Newcastle, Colorado. Photo 285 by H. S. Gale, courtesy USGS

mud gradually compacted and became hard rock, the buried carcasses were flattened into dark carbonized films. Fossilization in this manner can also preserve an animal's soft parts, which are not as well preserved in limestone.

Sediments like coarse marine sandstones generally are not as fossiliferous as limestones and shales, probably because a high influx of these sediments into the ocean tends to choke bottom-dwelling organisms. Therefore, areas with active sediment deposition are usually devoid of all but the most sparsely populated bottom dwellers. However, under certain conditions of catastrophic flooding or submarine slides, entire communities might be buried within a layer of sandstone.

Sandstones can provide excellent terrestrial fossils and imprints (Figure 122) and faithfully record the passage of animals by their fossil footprints, especially those of large dinosaurs. These are best made by deep impressions in moist sand that are filled with sediment such as windblown sand and later buried and lithified into sandstone. Subsequent erosion exposes layers of sandstone, and the softer material that originally filled the depression weathers out, often exposing a clear set of footprints.

MINERAL-BEARING ROCKS

Most minerals that form crystals of collectible size are found in igneous rocks, some are found in sedimentary rocks, and a few are found in metamorphic rocks. Many metallic ore mines are excavated in igneous rocks; therefore, these rocks are a major source of the mineral wealth throughout the world. Most igneous rocks are aggregates of two or more minerals. For example, granite is composed almost entirely of quartz and feldspar with a minor constituent of other minerals. Granitic rocks formed deep inside the crust, and crystal growth was controlled by the cooling rate of the magma and the available space.

Large crystals probably formed late in the crystallization of a large magma body such as a batholith. They also might form in the presence of volatiles such as water and carbon dioxide, permitting large crystals to grow in a small magma body such as a dike. As the magma body slowly cooled, possibly over a period of a million years or more, the crystals were able to grow directly out of the fluid melt or out of the volatile magmatic fluids that invaded the surrounding rocks.

If a granitic rock develops very large crystals, it is called a pegmatite, which is the major

Figure 123   A large feldspar crystal in pegmatite in a quarry near Glastonbury, Harford County, Connecticut. The faces have been painted to set them off. Photo 141 by E. S. Bastin, courtesy USGS

source for single-mineral crystals throughout the world. Granite pegmatites are known for their crystals of enormous size. They also contain rare minerals with smaller crystals. The granite associated with pegmatites often consists of quartz rods in a matrix of feldspar combined in a curious interlocking angular pattern that resembles Egyptian cuneiform writing. For this reason, it is called graphic granite and is an attractive rock found in large quantities where pegmatites are known to exist. Therefore, these rocks are a key for locating pegmatite deposits.

Pegmatite bodies are usually dikelike (tabular), lens-shaped, or consist of massive blobs within the parent rock. They range in length from a few inches to several hundred feet, and exceptional pegmatites have been traced for several miles. Pegmatites can be found in many localities, where well-exposed granite outcrops exist. But they are especially prevalent in the eastern and the mountainous western regions of the United States.

Figure 124 Stalactites in Carlsbad Caverns, Eddy County, New Mexico. Photo 2529 by W. T. Lee, courtesy USGS

Ordinary pegmatites are composed mainly of great masses of quartz and microcline, or potassium, feldspar (Figure 123), which are the dominant minerals in granite. Individual crystals range from a fraction of an inch to colossal size, weighing many tons. Quartz crystals have been found weighing thousands of pounds. Microcline crystals from Maine were reported to be up to 20 feet across. Some pegmatites might contain huge booklike segregations of mica over 10 feet wide. Also, large crystals of plagioclase, or sodium, feldspar called albite might be present in a tabular or platy form.

Extraordinary pegmatites contain a gamut of minerals in large crystals of which beryl, tourmaline, topaz, and fluorite are the most common. Many minerals, such as apatite, monazite, and zircon, that normally form only microscopic crystals in granite form especially large crystals in pegmatites. Pegmatites are mined extensively in many parts of the world for their large feldspar crystals, which are used in the ceramics industry. In the Karelia region of the Soviet Union, thousands of tons of feldspar were mined from several gigantic crystals, possibly the largest in the world.

Other industrial minerals, including radioactive ores, are mined from pegmatites. In addition, numerous gemstones and the so-called rare-earth elements, which are important for making superconductors, are associated with pegmatites. Some crystals in these rocks also reach enormous size. Spodumene crystals found in the Black Hills of South Dakota were over 40 feet long. Beryl crystals from Albany, Maine measured as much as 27 feet long and 6 feet wide.

Volcanoes provide numerous samples of diverse welded tuffs composed of volcanic ash, agglomerates, and ignimbrites (recrystallized ash flows) that are readily obtained by the collector. Ancient lava flows might contain clear, dark green, or black natural glass called obsidian. Some lava flows might contain cavities or vesicles that are filled with crystals called zeolites, meaning "boiling stones," because they formed when water boiled away as the basalt cooled. Trachytes, volcanic glass of basaltic composition, often contain large, well-shaped feldspar crystals that are aligned in the direction of the lava flow. Serpentine, so named because it often has the mottled green color of a serpent, is soft and easily polished, which enables it to be worked into a variety of ornaments and decorative objects.

Calcite, composed of calcium carbonate, is chief among the minerals precipitated from seawater. Under certain conditions, calcite can form large, lustrous crystals. One of the largest calcite crystals was from Sterling Bush, New York, and measured 43 inches long and weighed about half a ton. Calcite can grow in cavities to form long, tapering crystals that resemble dog's teeth, called dogtooth spar.

In limestone caves, long "icicles" of calcite grow from the ceiling down and from the floor up to form stalactites and stalagmites, respectively (Figure 124). Mineral springs produce layered deposits of calcium carbonate called travertine, which due to its numerous cavities resembles Swiss

Figure 125   Gypsum crystals in carbonaceous shale bed, Powder River County, Montana. Photo 92 by C. E. Dobbin, courtesy USGS

cheese. Crystals of a particularly clear form of calcite have optical qualities and have been used in petrographic, or rock, microscopes and aircraft bombsights.

Thick beds of gypsum, composed of hydrous calcium sulfate, constitute one of the most common sedimentary rocks (Figure 125). They formed in evaporite deposits, which occur when a pinched-off portion of the ocean or an inland sea evaporated. Oklahoma, which like many parts of the interior of North America that was invaded by a Mesozoic sea, is well known for its gypsum beds. Evaporite deposits contain large amounts of halite as well and are mined extensively throughout the world for this mineral. Gypsum is mainly used for the manufacture of plaster of paris and wallboard. It often develops into large, chevron-shaped double crystals called swallowtail twins. When gypsum is heated or compressed, water is driven off, and the mineral becomes anhydrite, which can revert to gypsum in the presence of water. If massive gypsum is compacted, it forms alabaster, which is often carved into vases and ornaments.

Sedimentary rocks frequently contain concretions, which are mineralized nodules. They occur in a variety of shapes, sizes, and colors. If the nodules are hollow and are lined with agate or various other crystals, they form geodes. When cut open, geodes reveal small, bright crystals or bands of colorful agate (Figure 126). Geodes can also occur when crystals composed of opal or chalcedony fill large cavities in basalt and are called "thunder eggs." Geodes make beautiful specimens when cut and polished.

If clay derived from the weathering of feldspar is buried deep inside the Earth, the extreme temperatures and pressures can alter it into muscovite, garnet, and other metamorphic minerals. Metamorphism also takes place in contact with hot magma bodies that invade the crust, and for this reason it is called contact metamorphism. During the metamorphic process, minerals in either sedimentary or igneous rocks might undergo recrystallization, which forms larger crystals. Chemical changes might take place, in which new minerals are formed in the place of old ones. Among the minerals found in contact metamorphic zones that might be of interest to collectors are garnet, epidote, and diopside.

COLLECTING FOSSILS AND MINERALS

Geology is one of the few scientific fields in which the amateur can still contribute substantially to its progress. Important discoveries are made all the time, not only by professional scientists but also by serious amateur geologists who seek the thrill of discovery. However, certain precautions must be observed. When exploring for fossils or minerals on national lands such as national parks, national monuments, national forests, wilderness areas, and public lands, or state lands, ask a park ranger whether any restrictions apply. Also, if collecting on private land, obtain permission from the landowner or mine owner. In addition, some states require a permit to collect fossils.

It is particularly important that sites where scientific work is being conducted be avoided. There are organizations that offer field trips for those interested in paleontology but have no formal training. Some museums and parks even allow visitors to take part in paleontologic digs. Also, in remote parts of the world, volunteer workers contribute substantially to scientific research.

Figure 126   Types of silica-lined geodes from green glass. At left is a geode with opal and chalcedony; center is a Dugway geode weathered from green glass and rounded by rolling on beaches; right is the interior of a Dugway geode showing banded agate and the hollow center lined with drusy quartz crystals. Photo 108 by M. H. Staatz, courtesy USGS

The search first begins by visiting the local library. Many libraries have published materials, including geologic road guides, other detailed guidebooks, and hobby books to acquaint the novice with the practicalities of fossil and rock collecting. The division of mines of most states, the U.S. Bureau of Mines, the U.S. Geological Survey, and the Bureau of Land Management might provide additional information. Many colleges and universities have geology departments that can assist the amateur collector. Natural history museums contain a wealth of information. Word of mouth from other collectors is also a good source of information. Often, rock shops are excellent places for purchasing books and equipment and obtaining information on the best sites for collecting.

Little equipment is required for successful rock collecting, and it might be found lying around the house or bought from hardware stores. A map, compass, notebook, and perhaps a field guide might come in handy for locating a collecting site. A geologist's pick or a bricklayer's hammer, and a sizable chisel can be used for breaking and splitting rocks. A trowel or a large knife can be used for splitting shale. A sledgehammer, shovel, and pry bar might come in handy for excavating rock. A sieve or strainer can be used for sifting loose sediments. A hand lens or a magnifying glass might be required for observing minute specimens. A paintbrush, toothbrush, or whisk broom can be used for sweeping clean the work space. A knapsack

Figure 127   Limestone quarry in Franklin County, Alabama.   Photo 1721 by E. F. Burchard, courtesy USGS

TABLE 11   FOSSILS BY STATE

Fossil specimens of these animals and plants can be found in relative abundance in the states listed.

Ammonites
Alabama
Alaska
Arkansas
California
Illinois
Kansas
Montana
Nebraska
Nevada
New Jersey
Oklahoma
Oregon
South Dakota
Texas
Mississippi
Missouri
West Virginia

Coral
Alabama
California
Georgia
Illinois
Michigan
Mississippi
New York
Pennsylvania
Texas
Virginia
West Virginia

Brachiopods
Alabama
Arkansas
California
Colorado
Georgia
Idaho
Iowa
Maine
Massachusetts
Missouri
Montana
Nebraska
New Hampshire
New Jersey
New York
Ohio
Oregon
Pennsylvania
Tennessee
Virginia
West Virginia

Crinoids
Colorado
Iowa
Missouri
Montana
New York
Oklahoma
Oregon
Pennsylvania
Texas
Virginia
West Virginia
Wyoming

Bryozoans
Alabama
Georgia
Nebraska
Pennsylvania
Texas
West Virginia

Dinosaurs
Arizona
Colorado
Connecticut
Massachusetts
Montana
New Jersey
New Mexico
Oklahoma
Tennessee
Texas
Utah
Wyoming

Cephalopods
Colorado
Delaware
Georgia
Michigan

Fish
Alaska
Arkansas
California
Connecticut
Kansas
Massachusetts
New Jersey
New York
Ohio
Texas
Virginia

Gastropods
Alabama
California
Colorado
Delaware
Georgia
Mississippi
Missouri
New Hampshire
Oregon
Pennsylvania
Tennessee
Texas
West Virginia

Graptolites
Alabama
Arkansas
Idaho
Maine
New York
Pennsylvania
Virginia
Washington

Insects
Alaska
California
Colorado
Illinois
Kansas
Montana
NewJersey
Oklahoma

Mammoths
Alaska
Florida
Nebraska
New York
South Dakota

Mastodons
Florida
Nevada
New Jersey
New York
Ohio

Mollusks
Alabama
Alaska
Massachusetts
Mississippi
New Jersey
New York
Oregon

Pelecypods
Alabama
Colorado
Delaware
Florida
Kansas
Louisiana
Mississippi
Missouri
Montana
Nebraska
Ohio
Pennsylvania
Texas
Virginia
Washington

Petrified wood
Arizona
California
Colorado
Idaho
Kansas
Montana
Nebraska
Nevada
Oklahoma
Oregon
South Dakota
Texas
Washington
Wyoming

Plants
Alabama
Arkansas
California
Colorado
Georgia
Illinois
Indiana
Iowa
Kansas
Kentucky
Massachusetts
Mississippi
Montana
New Mexico
North Carolina
North Dakota
Ohio
Oregon
Pennsylvania
Texas
Virginia
Washington
West Virginia

Shark's teeth
Alabama
Arkansas
California
Colorado
Florida
Maryland
Mississippi
New York
Oklahoma
Oregon
South Carolina

Trilobites
Alabama
California
Idaho
Illinois
Indiana
Iowa
Kansas
Massachusetts
Minnesota
Missouri
Nebraska
New Hampshire
New York
Ohio
Pennsylvania
Tennessee
Vermont
Virginia
Washington
West Virginia

Figure 128 Lillie and Vindicator Mines in Cripple Creek Mining District, Colorado, in 1903. Photo courtesy USGS

and various types of packing containers and newspaper for wrapping specimens can be used to safely transport collectibles home.

Because limestone is used in the manufacture of portland cement for building and road construction, limestone quarries dot the landscape across the country (Figure 127). In addition, building materials and gravel for roads are made from limestone, and limestone gravel pits are a common site in many parts of the nation.

Though caution should be used in the vicinity of any mine or pit, these quarries are often ideal sites for collecting fossils because many layers of limestone might be penetrated. In addition, the rocks have been conveniently broken up, exposing fresh surfaces, on which fossils, especially abundant shells, are clearly seen. Coal pits are also numerous and are excellent locations for collecting fossils of plants and animals that were buried in the great ancient coal swamps.

Abandoned ore mines, especially those in the West (Figure 128), are one of the best locations for collecting rocks and minerals, and, indeed, some of the best mineral specimens found in museums and in other collections were taken from mines. As mentioned, the largest crystals were discovered in mines that worked granite pegmatites. Open-pit mines provide large exposures of rock that can be explored for minerals. The waste dumps from abandoned underground mines are another excellent source for minerals. They are much safer than exploring the mines themselves, which are extremely dangerous and prone to caving and should be avoided. (A mine shaft might penetrate a particularly well crystallized zone on its way to a large amount of ore, and these rocks, which are of no use to the miners, end up in the waste dumps. Adjacent outcrops might also be mineralized and could yield valuable specimens.)

Road cuts are perhaps the most accessible locations for exploring for fossils and minerals because the collector can simply drive to them. Again, however, caution must be taken. When a road is constructed through hilly or mountainous terrain, often huge quantities of rock have to be blasted out, providing excellent exposures. Much of the geology across the country has been mapped using road cuts, railway cuts, and tunnels. If a road is cut through limestones or shales, fossils may be present. If a road is cut through igneous or metamorphic rocks, minerals, including some with sizable crystals, may be found.

Of lesser accessibility but with equally as good, if not better, rock exposures are stream channels, especially those that cut deep through hard rock. The Grand Canyon (Figures 129 and 130) provides perhaps the best example and is carved through rocks that are hundreds of millions of years old and over a mile thick. Well exposed sediment layers tell a nearly complete story about the geologic history of the Earth. On the bottom of the canyon lies the ancient original basement rock, upon which sediments

Figure 129   A view of the Grand Canyon from Mohave Point. Photo by George A. Grant, courtesy National Park Service

were slowly deposited layer upon layer. Even less spectacular stream channels can uncover exposures of rock that have no other access.

The easiest fossil collecting is in areas where specimens have been weathered out of the rock and lie in loose sediment or rocky debris, called scree or float, at the base of an exposure. Often the limestone encasing a fossil erodes more easily, leaving whole specimens scattered on the ground. Broken-up rock in abandoned limestone quarries might also provide good hand samples that contain abundant fossils. A rock containing a desirable fossil might have to be chiseled out of a large boulder. However, great care should be exercised when attempting to remove a fossil specimen from hard rock so that you do not crack or crumble it and thus destroy what nature has preserved for millions of years.

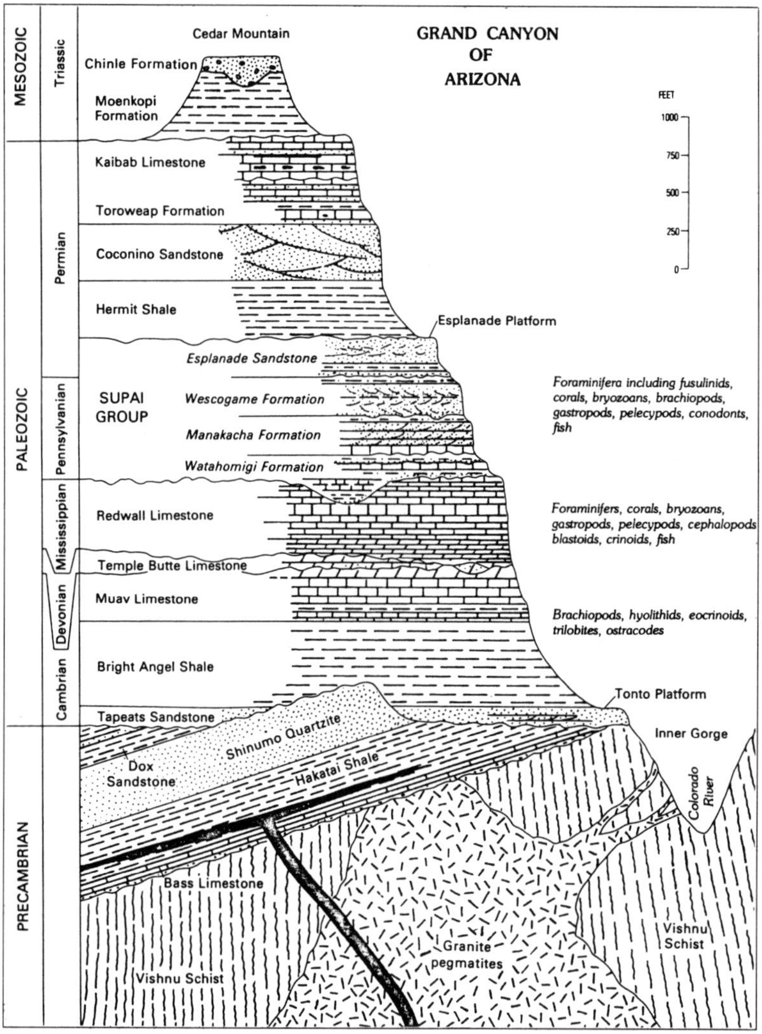

Figure 130   A cutaway view of rock bed formations that comprise the Supai Group of the Grand Canyon, Arizona. Courtesy U.S. Department of the Interior

GLOSSARY

abyssal of the deep ocean, generally over a mile in depth

agate a fine-grained variety of quartz composed of varicolored bands of chalcedony, usually occurring within rock cavities

amber fossil tree resin that has achieved a stable state after ground burial, through chemical change and the loss of volatile constituents

amphibian a cold-blooded, four-footed vertebrate, belonging to a class that is midway in evolutionary development between fishes and reptiles. Amphibians breathe by means of gills in the early stages of life and by means of lungs in the adult state.

amphiboles a group of common rock-forming minerals that occur most frequently in igneous and metamorphic rocks

angiosperms flowering plants which reproduce sexually

anion a negatively charged ion

annelid any wormlike invertebrate belonging to the phylum Annelida, characterized by a segmented body with a distinct head and appendages

arthropod a large group of invertebrates, including trilobites, crustaceans, and insects, characterized by segmented bodies, jointed appendages, and an exoskeleton or carapace of chitin

asteroid	one of many rocky or metallic bodies orbiting the sun between Mars and Jupiter. Asteroids are believed to once have been part of larger bodies that subsequently disintegrated.
axis	a straight line about which a body rotates. Also, a reference direction in crystals that is parallel to symmetry directions or the intersection of faces
basalt	a volcanic rock which is dark in color and usually quite fluid in the molten state
basement	the surface beneath which sedimentary rocks are not found; the igneous metamorphic, granitized, or highly deformed rock underlying sedimentary rocks
batholith	the largest of intrusive igneous bodies, more than 40 square miles on its uppermost surface
bivalve	marine and freshwater mollusk having a shell composed of two hinged valves; including oysters, mussels, clams, and other species
bomb, volcanic	a solidified blob of molten rock ejected from a volcano
brachiopod	marine invertebrates that live attached to a firm substratum in shallow waters. With bivalve shells, they have an appearance similar to mollusks. More plentiful in Paleozoic times, they now constitute a small phylum, including the lamp shells.
bryozoan	a marine invertebrate, characterized by a branching or fanlike structure, that grows in colonies. The skeleton may be chitinous or calcareous, but only the latter are found in fossil form.
calcareous	a substance containing calcium carbonate
carat	the standard unit of gem weight (mass); 1 carat = 0.2 gram
carbonization	the process of fossilization found most often in plants. During decomposition of the organic matter under water or sediment, hydrogen, oxygen, and nitrogen are exhausted, leaving a carbon residue that may retain many of the features of the original organism. This process resulted in the formation of the great coal deposits during the Carboniferous period, beginning at least 340 million years ago.

cation   a positively charged ion

chalcedony   a variety of quartz, having a compact fibrous structure and waxy luster, often found as a deposit, lining, or filling in rocks

chalk   a soft, earthy, fine-grained white to grayish limestone of marine origin, composed almost entirely of biochemically derived calcite that is formed mainly by shallow-water accumulations of minute plants and animals

chert   a dense, extremely hard siliceous sedimentary rock, consisting mainly of interlocking quartz crystals

chitin   a nitrogenous material. The outer covering of arthropods, the cuticle, is impregnated with chitin, which makes the exoskeleton more rigid, yielding a tough yet light and flexible waterproof skeleton; also found in the hard parts of several other groups of animals.

chondrule   a small globular body of various materials found in certain stony meteorites

class   in systematics, the category of plants and animals between phylum and order; a class comprises several orders

clastic   pertaining to sediment or rock composed mainly of fragments (clasts) derived from a preexisting, larger rock mass

cleavage   the tendency of a mineral to break along a plane due to a direction of weakness in the crystal

coelenterate   more developed than the Porifera, these multicelled organisms (including the corals) appeared during the early Cambrian and are widely distributed

conglomerate   a sedimentary rock composed of welded fine-grained and coarse-grained rock fragments

continent   a slab of light, granitic rock which floats on denser rocks of the upper mantle

continental shelf the offshore area of a continent in shallow sea

continental slope the transition from the continental margin to the deep-sea basin

coral   any of a large group of shallow-water, bottom-dwelling marine invertebrates; they make up the majority of fossilized remains

Coriolis effect	the apparent force that deflects the wind or a moving object and causes it to curve in relation to the rotation of the Earth
correlation	the determination of geologic age by comparing fossils from different times and regions
craton	the ancient, stable interior region of a continent, usually composed of the oldest rocks on the continent, commonly Precambrian
Cretaceous-Tertiary boundary	see K-T boundary
crustaceans	any arthropod of the subphylum Crustacea, characterized chiefly by two pairs of antennalike appendages in front of the mouth and three pairs behind it; includes shrimp, crabs, and lobsters
crystal	a solid body having a regularly repeating arrangement of its atomic constituents; the external expression may be bounded by natural planar surfaces called faces
Curie point	the temperature at which iron molecules align to a magnetic field upon cooling
density	the amount of any quantity per unit volume
diatom	any of numerous microscopic unicellular marine or freshwater algae having siliceous cell walls
dike	a body of intrusive igneous rock that cuts across the layering or structural fabric of the host rock
dolomite	see dolomitization
dolomitization	the process by which limestone becomes dolomite by the substitution of magnesium for the original calcite; common in organisms whose original hard parts were composed of calcite or aragonite, such as corals, brachiopods, and echinoderms
echinoderms	a phylum of marine invertebrates (including starfish, sea urchins, and sea cucumbers), some of which first appeared in the early Cambrian
effervescence	the bubbling reaction of hydrochloric acid on a carbonate rock

electron microscope	an instrument in which a beam of electrons is focused by magnetic fields to form an enlarged image of an object on a fluorescent screen
eolian	pertaining to or caused by wind, or a deposit of wind-blown sediment
eon	on the geologic time scale, the longest unit of time, composed of several eras
epoch	an interval of geologic time longer than an age and shorter than a period
era	on the geologic time scale, the unit of time below eon; composed of several periods
erosion	the wearing away of any part of the Earth's surface by natural agencies
eukaryote	an organism sufficiently developed so that the genetic material (DNA) is enclosed by membranes, forming a nucleus; compare to prokaryote
evaporite	minerals and sediment deposited from a saline solution, usually seawater, as it evaporates
exoskeleton	the hard outer covering of the body of certain animals, such as the thick cuticle of insects and crustaceans or the shell of mollusks, protecting the internal organs and supporting the body
external mold	impression of the exterior of an organism's shell left on sediment when the shell and other organic material have dissolved
extinctions	the loss of a large number of species over a short geologic period
extrusive	any igneous volcanic rock which is ejected onto the surface of the Earth; compare to intrusive
face	on a crystal, one of the planar bounding surfaces
family	in systematics, the category of plants and animals between order and genus; a family is composed of several genera
fault	a break in the rocks due to crustal motion
feldspar	a group of rock-forming minerals that make up about 60% of the Earth's crust. They occur in all types of rock, but are essential constituents of most igneous rocks.

filament	a narrow threadlike structure; in algae, a line of similar cells joined by their end walls
fissile	the ability of a rock to split into thin sheets
fissure	a large crack in the crust through which magma might escape from a volcano
flagella	whiplike appendages used to propel organisms
fluorescence	the property of emitting light as a result of absorbing light
fluvial	of or pertaining to rivers and streams
foliation	a planar arrangement of the textural or structural features in any variety of rock
foraminifera	calcium carbonate secreting organisms that live in the surface waters of the oceans; after death, their shells fall to the seafloor where they form the primary constituents of limestone. They are the most common marine protozoa found in fossil form.
fossil	any remains, impression, or trace in rock of a plant or animal of a previous geologic age
fulgurite	glassy tubes of lightning-fused rock, most common on mountain tops
gastropod	a large class of mollusks, including slugs, snails, and others, characterized by a well-developed head with tentacles and eyes, a single shell (often coiled), and a large flat foot. None of the gastropods are attached to the substrate; some forms are air breathing and adapted to terrestrial habitats.
genus	in systematics, the category of plants and animals between family and species; a genus is composed of several species
geode	a hollow, globular mineral body that can develop in limestone and lavas. Its usual shape is nearly spherical.
geosyncline	a basinlike or elongated subsidence of the Earth's crust. Its length may extend for several thousand miles and may contain sediments thousands of feet thick, representing millions of years of deposits. A geosyncline generally forms along continental edges, and is destroyed during periods of crustal deformation.

glaciation   the covering of the Earth's surface by glaciers, sheets of glowing ice. In the Earth's history, periods of glaciation (ice ages) have alternated with warmer intervals (interglacials).

gneiss   a banded, coarse-grained metamorphic rock with alternating layers of unlike minerals. It consists of essentially the same components as granite.

gradualism   a theory that geologic processes operated in the past as they do today. Also known as uniformitarianism

granite   a coarse-grained, silica-rich rock consisting primarily of quartz and feldspars. It is the principal constituent of the continents and is believed to be derived from a molten state beneath the Earth's surface.

granitic rocks   igneous rocks formed by magma intrusion into the crust

greenstone   a more or less overall term for any green, weakly metamorphosed igneous rock

gypsum   a common, widely distributed mineral, frequently associated with halite

halite   a mineral that occurs most commonly in bedded deposits. It is the most abundant of the evaporites, following gypsum and anhydrite in the sequence of precipitation of salts from seawater.

hard parts   those parts of an organism, such as the shell, skeleton, bones, and teeth that resist decay. Usually made of silica, chitin, calcium carbonate, or keratin, they make up the majority of fossilized remains.

hexagonal   in the crystal system it is defined by three equal axes lying in a plane and intersecting at 120-degree angles and a fourth perpendicular axis that is a sixfold rotation

hydrate   a compound produced by the chemical combination of water with another substance, or one in which water is a constituent of the chemical composition

hydrothermal   relating to the movement of hot water through the Earth's crust

igneous   rock that comprises the Earth's crust, formed of hardened magma

ignimbrite   volcanic deposits created by ejections of incandescent solid particles

index fossil	a representative fossil that allows paleontologists to identify those strata in which it is found; also called facies fossil and guide fossil
interglacial period	the warmer periods of time between glaciations (ice ages)
internal mold	the impression of the inside of an organism's shell. An internal mold results when a shell becomes filled with sediment and then dissolves, leaving the impression.
intertidal zones	the shore zone between high and low tides
intrusive	any igneous body which has solidified in place below the surface of the Earth; compare to extrusive
invertebrates	animals with external skeletons such as shellfish and insects
ionic bonding	the bonding of atoms by electrical charges due to the loss or gain of electrons
iridescence	color produced by light interference
kimberlite pipes	diamond-bearing pipelike structures in South Africa. The pipes are known as diatremes, and are formed deep within the Earth's crust by the explosion of magmatic gases or heated groundwater.
kinetic energy	the energy that a moving body possesses as a consequence of its motion
K-T boundary	the boundary formation marking the end of the dinosaur era
lacustrine	pertaining to lakes, as in a lacustrine environment
lapilli	a term interchangeable with cinder, which are small, solid pyroclastic fragments
lava	molten magma after it has flowed out onto the surface
leach (out)	the dissolution of soluble substances in rocks by the percolation of meteoric water
limestone	a sedimentary rock composed of calcium carbonate that is secreted from seawater by invertebrates whose skeletons composed the bulk of deposits
lithification	the conversion of unconsolidated sediments into a solid rock
loess	a deep deposit of airborne dust

macrofossil — a fossil large enough to be examined with the naked eye; compare to microfossil

magma — a molten rock material generated within the Earth, it is the constituent of igneous rocks, including volcanic eruptions

mammals — higher, warm-blooded vertebrates that give live births and are generally covered with hair or fur

mantle — the part of the Earth below the crust and above the core, composed of dense iron-magnesium-rich rocks

margin — in plate tectonics, the seam where two plates collide; the plates may slide past each other, or one may slide over another

marsupials — primitive, warm-blooded animals that wean their young in a belly pouch

metallic — the property of a substance exhibiting the characteristics of a metal

metamorphic rock — a rock crystallized from previous igneous, metamorphic, or sedimentary rocks created under conditions of intense temperatures and pressures without melting

metazoans — primitive multicellular animals whose cells have differentiated for various functions

meteorite — a metallic or stony body from space that enters the Earth's atmosphere and impacts on the Earth's surface

microfossil — fossil remains so small that a microscope is necessary to observe them; compare to macrofossil

Mohs scale — a standard of 10 minerals by which mineral hardness may be rated. On a scale of 1 to 10, from softest to hardest: talc, gypsum, calcite, fluorite, apatite, orthoclase, quartz, topaz, corundum, diamond.

mold — an impression of a fossil shell or other organic structure made in the encasing material

mollusks — a very large phylum of invertebrates, characterized by an internal or external shell surrounding a soft body; appearing during the early Cambrian, mollusks are known to paleontologists almost exclusively by their shells

monoclinic	in the crystal system it is defined by three nonparallel axes where there are only two right angles between the axes and no high-order rotation axes
moraine	a ridge of erosional debris deposited by the melting margin of a glacier
noncarbonate rocks	rocks whose composition excludes carbonate
nonfoliated rocks	rocks without layers, having a massive structure
nonmetallic	describes all substances that are not metals
ophiolite	masses of igneous rocks, such as basalt, whose structure and composition identify them as segments of ocean crust pushed into the continents by plate collisions
ore	a naturally occurring material from which a valuable mineral can be extracted
orogeny	an episode of mountain building
orthorhombic	(crystal system) defined by three unequal mutually perpendicular axes
paleomagnetism	the study of changes in the Earths' geomagnetic field
Pangaea	an ancient supercontinent that included all the landmass of the Earth
parallel faults	multiple faults aligned in the same direction. Also called echelon faults
pegmatite	an igneous rock with conspicuously large mineral grains, often enriched with volatile elements
period	a division of geologic time longer than an epoch and included in an era
permafrost	permanently frozen ground
petrified wood	silicified wood, formed by the silica permineralization of wood in such a manner that the original shape and structural detail are preserved
petrographic microscope	an instrument for magnifying rocks
photosynthesis	the process by which plants create carbohydrates from carbon dioxide, water, and sunlight

phylum   in zoologic classification, the category between king-dom and class

placoderm   an extinct class of chordates, fish with armorlike plates and articulated jaws

plagioclase   a group of triclinic feldspars

plate tectonics   the theory that accounts for the major features of the Earth's surface in terms of the interaction of lithospheric plates. See tectonics.

polarity   a condition in which a substance exhibits opposite properties such as electrical charges or magnetism

polygons   a geometric shape with three or more sides

polyhedron   a solid formed by plane faces

polyp   the tubular-shaped body of hydrozoans and coelenter-ates; polyps may form branching colonies or may break off, in the process of budding, to form new organisms

precipitate   a substance separated from a solution

primary rocks   ancient parent rocks from which younger rocks formed

prokaryote   a primitive organism lacking a nucleus

protistids   unicellular organisms, including bacteria, protozoans, algae, and fungus

pterosaur   an extinct order of flying reptiles, with leathery wings

pyroxene   a group of common rock-forming minerals

quartzite   a metamorphic rock consisting primarily of quartz grains, formed by the recrystallization of sandstone by thermal or regional metamorphism. Also, a sandstone composed of quartz grains cemented by silica

radial symmetry   a pattern of symmetry in which similar parts of an organism are arranged about an axis or central point, as in a starfish

radioactivity   an atomic reaction releasing detectable radioactive par-ticles

radiocarbon dating   a method of dating fossil remains by determining the amount of carbon isotopes in a given element

radiometric dating   a method of dating fossil remains by the testing of stable versus unstable radioactive material

red beds	predominately red sedimentary strata composed primarily of sandstone, siltstone, and shale; their color is due to the presence of ferric oxide
refraction	the bending of light (or any wave phenomenon) when it moves between media with different conductive velocities
relative dating	the chronological arrangement of rocks without references to actual ages
reptiles	air-breathing, cold-blooded animals that lay eggs and are generally covered by scales
sandstone	a sedimentary rock consisting of sand grains cemented together
schist	a finely layered metamorphic rock that tends to split readily into thin flakes
seafloor spreading	the theory that the ocean floor is created by the separation of lithospheric plates along the midocean ridges, with new oceanic crust formed from mantle material that rises from the mantle to fill the rift
sediment	the debris, organic or inorganic, transported and deposited by wind, water, or ice. It may form loose sediment, like sand or mud, or become consolidated to form sedimentary rock.
sedimentary gaps	a lack of continuity in the stratigraphic record, caused by a weathering or erosion of surface before new layers are deposited; also called an unconformity
sedimentation	the process by which sediment is formed, transported, and deposited
shale	a fine-grained sedimentary rock formed by the compaction of silt, clay, or sand that accumulate in river deltas and on lake and ocean bottoms. It is the most abundant of all sedimentary rock.
shard	a fragment, such as from broken pottery. Also, small glassy volcanic fragment
shield	areas of the exposed Precambrian nucleus of a continent
sial	a lightweight layer of rock that lies below the continents
siliceous	referring to sand, rock, or other substance containing abundant silica (silicon dioxide)

sill   a tabular igneous intrusion with boundaries parallel to the planar structure of the surrounding rock

siltstone   a sedimentary rock composed of hardened silt, having the composition and texture of shale, but lacking its fine lamination. Siltstones are intermediate between sandstones and shales but less common than either.

sima   a dense rock which composes the ocean floor and on which the sial floats

soft parts   those parts of an animal, such as internal organs or tissues, that decompose rapidly after death and are rarely preserved in the fossil state

species   in systematics, the lowest classification, below genus; all members of a species share similar characteristics and are able to breed among themselves

specific gravity   a dimensionless measure of density (numerically equivalent to the value in grams per cubic centimeter)

spherules   small, spherical, glassy grains found on certain types of meteorites, lunar soils, and large meteorite impact sites on Earth

spores   unicellular bodies used for primitive reproduction

stalactites   conical or cylindrical mineral deposits, usually calcite, that hang from the ceilings of limestone caves and range in length from a fraction of an inch to several feet

stalagmites   mineral deposits, usually calcite, which are built by water dripping onto a limestone cave floor

stock   an intrusive body of deep-seated igneous rock, usually lacking conformity and resembling a batholith, except for its smaller size

strata   layered rock formations; also called beds

stratification   a pattern of layering in sedimentary rock, lava flows or water, or materials of different composition or density

stromatolite   sedimentary formation in the shape of cushions or columns produced by lime-secreting blue-green algae (cyanobacteria)

subduction zone   an area where the oceanic plate dives below a continental plate into the asthenosphere. Ocean trenches are the surface expression of a subduction zone.

supernova	an enormous stellar explosion in which all but the inner core of a star is blown off into interstellar space, producing as much energy in a few days as the sun does in a billion years
tectonic activity	the formation of the Earth's crust by large-scale Earth movements throughout geologic time
tectonics	in geology, the history of the larger features of the Earth (rock formations and plates) and the forces and movements that produce them. See plate tectonics.
tektites	small, glassy minerals created from the melting of surface rocks by an impact of a large meteorite
tephra	all clastic material from dust particles to large chunks, expelled from volcanoes during eruptions
Tethys Sea	the hypothetical midlatitude area of the oceans separating the northern and southern continents of Gondwana and Laurasia some hundreds of millions years ago
tetragonal	in the crystal system it is defined by three mutually perpendicular axes, two of which are of equal length
thecodont	the most ancient and most primitive order of reptiles, now extinct, which gave rise to all the other orders, including dinosaurs, crocodiles, and birds
thermophilic	describes primitive organisms that live in hot water environments
till	nonstratified material deposited directly by glacial ice as it recedes
tillite	a sedimentary rock formed by the compaction and cementation of till
trachyte	a fine-grained, extrusive alkaline rock approximately silica-saturated, and with a wide compositional range
transform fault	a fracture in the Earth's crust along which lateral movement occurs. They are common features of the midocean ridges, created in the line of seafloor spreading.
trend	the direction in which a geologic feature is aligned
triclinic	(crystal system) defined by a lack of symmetry other than a possible center; triclinic crystals are characterized by three unequal axes that are mutually oblique

trilobite	an extinct marine arthropod, characterized by a body divided into three lobes, each bearing a pair of jointed appendages, and a chitinous exoskeleton
tuff	a rock formed of pyroclastic fragments
valve	one of the two articulated parts (shells) of a bivalve mollusk or other organism
varves	annual deposits developed by cyclic sedimentation, often on the floors of cold freshwater lakes. Fine-textured, dark layers alternate with coarser-grained lighter layers in a banded sequence of couplets.
vein	a tabular or sheetlike body of one or more minerals deposited in openings of fissures, joints, or faults
vertebrates	animals with an internal skeleton such as fish, amphibians, reptiles, and mammals
viscosity	the resistance of a liquid to flow
volatiles	in a magma, those materials that readily form a gas and are the last to enter into, and crystallize as minerals during, solidification
volcanic rock	any extrusive rock and associated high-level intrusive rock. The group is entirely magmatic.
volcano	a fissure or vent in the crust through which molten rock rises to the surface to form a mountain
x-ray diffraction machine	a device used to identify crystals by scattering x-rays onto a photographic plate

BIBLIOGRAPHY

THE EARTH'S HISTORY

Bird, Peter. "Formation of the Rocky Mountains, Western United States: A Continuum Computer Model." *Science* 239 (March 25, 1988): 1501–1507.

Boucot, A. J., and Jane Gray. "A Paleozoic Pangaea." *Science* 222 (November 11, 1983): 571–580.

Eldredge, Niles. *Life Pulse: Episodes from the Story of the Fossil Record.* New York: Facts On File, 1987.

Kerr, Richard A. "How to Make a Warm Cretaceous Climate." *Science* 223 (February 17, 1984): 677–678.

Mintz, Leigh W. *Historical Geology: The Science of a Dynamic Earth.* Columbus: Charles E. Merrill, 1972.

Schopf, William J., and Bonnie M. Packer. "Early Archean (3.3-Billion to 3.5-Billion-Year-Old) Microfossils from Warrawona Group, Australia." *Science* 237 (July 3, 1987): 70–72.

Stokes, W. Lee. *Essentials of Earth History.* Englewood Cliffs, N.J.: Prentice-Hall, 1982.

Tarbuck, Edward J., and Frederick K. Lutgens. *Earth Science.* Columbus: Charles E. Merrill, 1982.

CLUES TO THE PAST

Alverez, Walter, et al. "Impact Theory of Mass Extinctions and the Invertebrate Fossil Record." *Science* 223 (March 16, 1984): 1135–1140.

Bakker, Robert T. "Evolution by Revolution." *Science* 85 (November 1985): 72–80.

Crowley, Thomas J., and Gerald R. North. "Abrupt Climate Change and Extinction Events in Earth History." *Science* 240 (May 20, 1988): 996–1001.

Ford, Trevor D. "Life in the Precambrian." *Nature* 285 (May 22, 1980): 193–194.

Herbert, Sandra. "Darwin as a Geologist." *Scientific American* 254 (May 1986): 116–123.

Lewin, Roger. "A Lopsided Look at Evolution." *Science* 241 (July 15, 1988): 291–293.

Raup, David M. "Biological Extinctions in Earth History." *Science* 231 (March 28, 1986): 1528–1533.

ROCK TYPES

Blatt, Harvey, Gerard Middleton, and Raymond Murray. *Origin of Sedimentary Rocks*. Englewood Cliffs, N.J.: Prentice-Hall, 1972.

Bowen, N. L. *Igneous Rocks*. New York: Dover, 1956.

Decker, Robert, and Barbara Decker. *Volcanoes*. San Francisco: Freeman, 1981.

Foster, Robert J. *Physical Geology*. Columbus: Charles E. Merrill, 1971.

Mathews, Robley K. *Dynamic Stratigraphy*. Englewood Cliffs, N.J.: Prentice-Hall, 1974.

Pearl, Richard M. *Rocks and Minerals*. New York: Barnes and Noble, 1969.

Ritchie, David. *The Ring of Fire*. New York: Atheneum, 1981.

White, Robert S., and Dan P. McKenzie. "Volcanism at Rifts." *Scientific American* 261 (July 1989): 62–71.

FOSSIL FORMATION

Beerbower, James R. *Search for the Past: An Introduction to Paleontology*. Englewood Cliffs, N. J.: Prentice-Hall, 1968.

Jeffery, David. "Fossils: Annals of Life Written in Rock." *National Geographic* 168 (August 1985): 182–191.

Lewin, Roger. "Statistical Traps Lurk in the Fossil Record." *Science* 236 (May 1, 1987): 521–522.

Mossman, David J., and William A. S. Sarjeant. "The Footprints of Extinct Animals." *Scientific American* 248 (January 1983): 75–85.

Ridley, Mark. "Evolution and Gaps in the Fossil Record." *Nature* 286 (July 31, 1980): 444–445.

MARINE FOSSILS

Goreau, Thomas F., Nora I. Goreau, and Thomas J. Goreau. "Corals and Coral Reefs." *Scientific American* 241 (August 1979): 124–136.

McMenamin, Mark A. S. "The Emergence of Animals." *Scientific American* 256 (April 1987): 94–102.

Morris, Simon Conway, and H. B. Whittington. "Animals of the Burgess Shale." *Scientific American* 241 (July 1979): 122–133.

Richardson, Joice R., "Brachiopods." *Scientific American* 255 (September 1986): 100–106.

Stanley, Steven M. "Mass Extinctions in the Ocean." *Scientific American* 250 (June 1984): 64–72.

Vogel, Shawna. "Face-To-Face with a Living Fossil." *Discover* 9 (March 1988): 56–57.

Ward, Peter. "The Extinction of the Ammonites." *Scientific American* 247 (October 1983): 136–147.

TERRESTRIAL FOSSILS

Buffetaut, Eric, and Rucha Ingavat. "The Mesozoic Vertebrates of Thailand." *Scientific American* 253 (August 1985): 80–87.

Emery, Kenneth. "Precursors of Mammals." *Science Digest* 90 (January 1982): 19.

Horner, John R. "The Nesting Behavior of Dinosaurs." *Scientific American* 250 (April 1984): 130–137.

Lewin, Roger. "On the Origin of Insect Wings." *Science* 230 (October 25, 1985): 428–429.

Monastersky, Richard. "Dinosaurs in the Dark." *Science News* 133 (March 19, 1988): 184–186.

Morell, Virginia. "Announcing the Birth of a Heresy." *Discover* 8 (March 1987): 26–50.

Shipman, Pat. "How a 125 Million-Year-Old Dinosaur Evolved in 160 Years." *Discover* (October 1986): 94–101.

Weisburd, Stefi. "Brushing up on Dinosaurs." *Science News* 130 (October 4, 1986): 216–219.

CRYSTALS AND MINERALS

Bottley, E. P. *Rocks and Minerals*. New York: G. P. Putnam's Sons, 1969.

Hazen, Robert M., and Larry W. Finger. "Crystals at High Pressure." *Scientific American* 252 (May 1985): 110–117.

Muecke, Gunter K., and Peter Moller. "The Not-So-Rare Earths." *Scientific American* 258 (January 1988): 72–77.

Nelson, David R. "Quasicrystals." *Scientific American* 255 (August 1986): 43–51.

Rona, Peter A. "Mineral Deposits from Sea-Floor Hot Springs." *Scientific American* 254 (January 1986): 84–92.

Witzke, Brian J. "Geodes from Iowa." *Earth Science* 41 (Summer 1988): 19.

Zim, Hubert S., and Paul R. Shaffer. *Rocks and Minerals.* New York: Golden Press, 1957.

GEMS AND PRECIOUS METALS

Bouer, Max. *Precious Stones.* Rutland, Vt.: Charles F. Tuttle, 1969.

Edward Cayce Foundation. *Gems and Stones.* Virginia Beach, Va.: A.R.E. Press, 1987.

Green, Timothy. "All That Glitters." *Modern Maturity* 31 (August/September 1988): 54–60.

Hurlbut, Cornelius S., Jr. *Dana's Manual of Mineralogy.* New York: Wiley, 1971.

Peterson, James A. *Finding and Preparing Precious and Semiprecious Stones.* New York: Association Press, 1974.

Wright, J. B. *Mineral Deposits, Continental Drift, and Plate Tectonics.* Montvale, N.J.: Dowden, 1973.

THE RARE AND UNUSUAL

Fisher, Arthur. "What Flips Earth's Field?" *Popular Science* 232 (January 1988): 71–74.

Peterson, Ivars. "Earthward on a Rocky, Chaotic Course." *Science News* 128 (July 13, 1985): 23.

Pittock, A. Barrie. "Cycles in the Precambrian." *Nature* 318 (December 12, 1985): 509–510.

Sharpton, Virgil L. "Glasses Sharpen Impact Views." *Geotimes* 33 (June 1988): 10–11.

Weisburd, Stefi. "Largest Melt from Lightning Strike." *Science News* 130 (October 11, 1986): 231.

———. "The Microbes That Loved the Sun." *Science News* 129 (February 15, 1986): 108–110.

———. "Self-Reversing Minerals Make a Comeback." *Science News* 127 (April 13, 1985): 234–236.

————. "Halos of Stone." *Science News* 127 (January 19, 1985): 42–44.

WHERE FOSSILS AND MINERALS ARE FOUND

Averett, Walter R. "Fertile Fossil Field." *Earth Science* 41 (Spring 1988): 16–18.

Bancroft, Peter. *The World's Finest Minerals and Crystals.* New York: Viking Press, 1973.

Colbert, Edwin H. *A Fossil Hunter's Notebook.* New York: E. P. Dutton, 1980.

Hannibal, Joseph T. "Quarries Yield Rare Paleozoic Fossils." *Geotimes* 33 (July 1988): 10–13.

Fisher, Louis J. "Finding Fossils." *Earth Science* 41 (Summer 1988): 20–22.

LaPlante, Jerry C. *The Weekend Fossil Hunter.* Orlando: Drake, 1977.

MacDonald, James R. *The Fossil Collector's Handbook.* Englewood Cliffs, N. J.: Prentice-Hall, 1983.

MacFall, Russell P. *Rock Hunter's Guide.* New York: Thomas Y. Crowell, 1980.

Pearl, Richard M. *Successful Mineral Collecting and Prospecting.* New York: Bonanza Books, 1961.

Sanborn, William B. *Crystal and Mineral Collecting.* Mentone, Calif.: Lane, 1960.

INDEX

INDEX

INDEX

INDEX